The Wonderful World of Wigglers

Written by
Julia Hand

Illustrated by
Carolyn Peduzzi

A Common Roots Guidebook

Library of Congress Catalog Card Number: 93-73783

ISBN: 1-884430-01-7

Author: Julia Hand

Editor: Carolyn Peduzzi

Illustrator: Carolyn Peduzzi

Book Design: Carolyn Peduzzi

Common Roots
A Framework For Integrated Living Curriculum

Social Studies
creative arts
language arts
math
gardening
community service
health \ nutrition
Science \ ecology

Dedicated to Wilma.

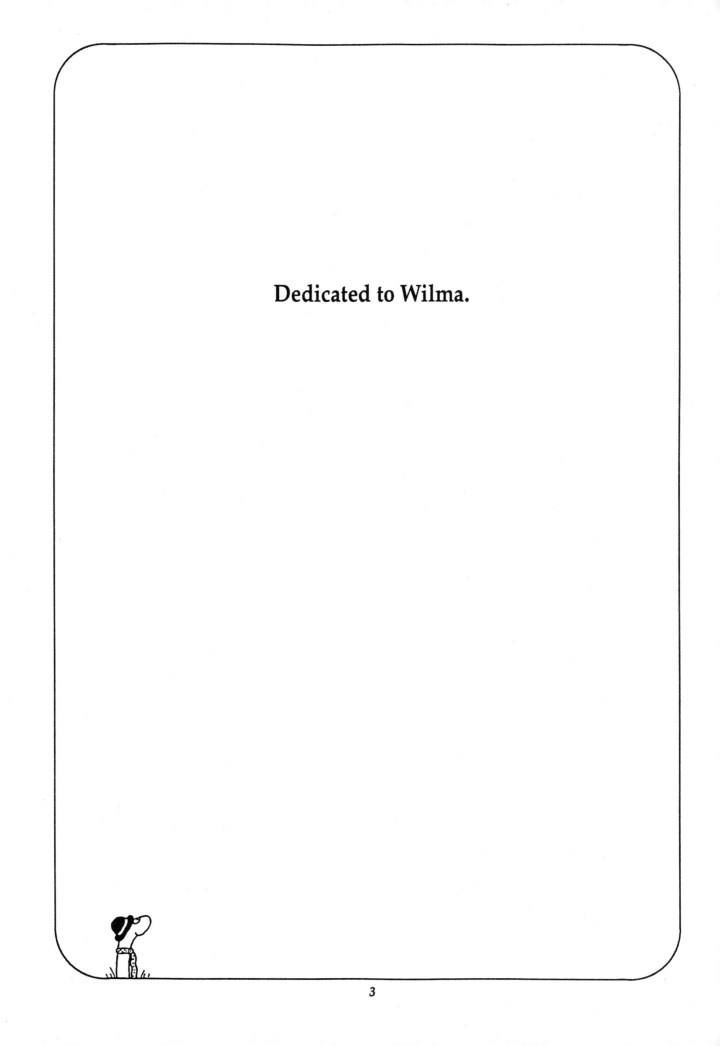

The Wonderful World of Wigglers

Table of Contents

Preface

For us at Food Works, and for literally hundreds of children, teachers, parents and community members, this *Common Roots™ Guidebook* represents far more than a collection of hands-on environmental activities for the young learner. For all of us, this Guide is a roadmap for placing schools back at the center of communities - by providing students with opportunities to address critical concerns in their neighborhoods, towns, surrounding countryside and larger world.

Food Works grew out of our community work attempting to unravel the spiral of hunger, poverty and ecological collapse locally and globally, from rural Vermont to rural Africa.

Through this work, we discovered that the very ways we learn about the endangered world both reflect and recreate that world. In elementary school, for example, we learned to divide up the world into neat categories - Math, Science, Social Studies and so forth. We then applied those same tools in adulthood to divide up the world— Politics, Economics, Environment, etc.— which has led to a patchwork of temporary band-aids rather than sustainable solutions to these endemic problems.

In trying to create a world that nourishes all forms of life, we must teach ourselves from the earliest ages to see the world as an interconnected whole of which we are an integral part. We at Food Works believe the purpose of schooling should be to nurture the natural curiosity, imagination and dreams of all children, in order to re-create a world capable of responding to the diverse spectrum of intellectual, emotional, creative and nutritional needs of all its inhabitants.

Common Roots provides the practical skills enabling our children to more holistically understand and explore the inter-relationships between the natural and human world. Therefore, we at Food Works have dedicated our work to transforming the role and responsibility of our schools in order to identify and respond to the food related and ecological concerns of our communities so that we may create a healthy future.

Joseph Kiefer

Acknowledgements

The *Common Roots*™ framework as a vehicle for re-inventing schools would not have been possible without the desire and enthusiasm of the many teachers, parents and children to change the way we look at the role of our schools.

The Rumney School was the first to offer us a school in which to pioneer the development of the *Common Roots* framework that included the K-6 Historic Theme Gardens.

The Barnet School hosted our first *Common Roots* graduate course, which taught us the critical importance of each teacher owning his or her unique journey for integrated learning. This collaborative relationship continues to grow and bear fruit.

Additionally, we would like to thank all of our new schools and the unique way they have adopted *Common Roots* to meet their needs.

Unquestionably, none of this would have been possible without the dedication and vision of the Food Works collaborative team. The rich insights and personal teaching experiences of Julia Hand, JoAnne Dennee, Elisheva Kaufman, Carolyn Peduzzi, Jack Peduzzi, and Joseph Kiefer have inspired the genesis of *Common Roots*.

The guidance and support of our Board of Directors has been instrumental in sustaining the *Common Roots* vision. Their collective wisdom is a constant source of inspiration and direction.

Most importantly, we would like to acknowledge the many family and foundation funders whose generous support has enabled us to realize our common dream. By believing in our vision and continuing to support this evolving work, this group of friends has become part of our growing Food Works family.

Above all, listening to the voices of children has taught us the timely need to provide meaningful opportunities for them to create a better world.

Introduction to
The Wonderful World of Wigglers

A Common Roots Guidebook

Welcome!

The Wonderful World of Wigglers emphasizes the crucial relationship between earthworms, the health of the soil, and sustainability. If we wish to live an ecologically sustainable life style - indeed, if we wish to continue feeding ourselves - we need to nourish and build the soil.

Each year, the United States loses 1.7 billion pounds of soil. In some places, over a century of soil building can be lost in 10 years. Moreover, the fertilizers, herbicides, and insecticides we add to the soil further deplete its life-giving properties. Darwin, who devoted much of his life to studying earthworms, discovered that nutrient-rich earthworm castings can contribute as much as 2/10 of an inch of soil per acre in a single year.

Though the Earth is quite frozen in winter, soil can be brought alive in the classroom through the Earthworm Compost Farm. *The Wonderful World of Wigglers* may be used as a guide to explore the amazing world of earthworms by any child in any grade. It is filled with integrated activities and projects that will challenge children to solve real-life problems through critical and creative thinking.

Children learn how to use the applied scientific method and guided inquiry to motivate investigations, design experiments, and directly apply their knowledge. Additionally, the guidebook includes tangible and meaningful projects to benefit the child's school and community.

The Wonderful World of Wigglers makes a direct connection between soil ecology, growing food, and community. This guidebook provides hands-on activities that foster these connections and develop an appreciation for and understanding of the role of earthworms in the soil community.

This project begins with a *student inquiry*, which guides the investigations. Some examples of essential questions might include

- What do I know about earthworms?
- What do earthworms do?

- Where do earthworms live?
- Are earthworms important? Why?
- What can I do to help earthworms?
- Are there different kinds of earthworms?
- How are earthworms connected to the larger ecosystems?
- Why is the health of the soil community important to the health of the human community?

Inquiry can inspire children to seek answers to questions they may have about the world. Documenting these questions fosters a student-centered approach. This list can then be used to help guide students' investigations. It's very possible that children just might discover something no one else knows about earthworms!

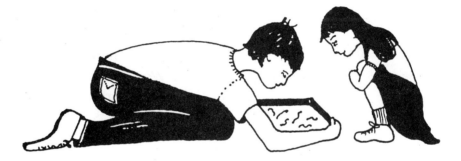

How can earthworms inspire caring and respect for the world around us?

An Earthworm Compost Farm can be a powerful outlet for children who feel an ethical responsibility to heal the earth community. Children can actively help to enrich the soil by keeping and caring for earthworms. Earthworms are a vital link to the soil-building process because they ingest organic material and create fertile, rich vermicompost with their droppings.

Learning to appreciate the simple wonder of the earthworm can be a critical step toward understanding the delicate complexity of the planet. Sometimes, when we encounter something that is new and mysterious, especially if it is different and we don't like the way it looks, we tend to judge it as something bad. But if we familiarize ourselves with this new and different thing, be it human or earthworm, an openness occurs. Judgment gives way to respect and appreciation for the importance of diversity. And diversity is the key to the health of the planet.

The *Wonderful World of Wigglers* sets a tone that reflects an attitude of gentleness and respect for earthworms. These miraculous creatures of the soil are seen as living beings with a nervous system, hearts, and blood much like ours. Such a view engenders compassion and acceptance, not only for earthworms, but for all life. When we can walk upon the Earth with awareness for those that lie beneath our feet, we may begin to move in a different way, with refreshing sensitivity and promise, and peace in every step.

Organization of *The Wonderful World of Wigglers*

This guidebook is divided into nine chapters, each of which investigates the earthworm and its place in the world. These chapters include:

1 *Meeting the wondrous, wiggly worm.*
2 *Building an Earthworm Compost Farm.*
3 *Appreciating the magic that these peaceful wigglers work, and how this benefits human communities.*
4 *Investigating the intricate mysteries of the earthworm, inside and out.*
5 *Exploring the earthworm's life cycle.*
6 *Who's who in the Earthworm Compost Farm Community.*
7 *Making earthworm high-rise apartment houses for each students desk.*
8 *Comparing and contrasting the compost process with the Earthworm Compost Farm.*
9 *Putting it all together with culminating activities and projects.*

Like a food web, all the activities interconnect, and many of them build upon one another. Throughout the *Wonderful World of Wigglers* you will find activities that provide opportunities to weave the creative arts, language arts, social studies, science and math into your explorations of the earthworm community.

Student Discovery Sheets guide investigations. These can be xeroxed and passed out to students. The "Explorations and Experiments" Discovery Sheet (page 52) may be used as a model for students wishing to conduct their own experiments.

You will also find examples of extension activities designed to supplement many of the important concepts. It is hoped that these activities and projects will be flexible enough to address unique learning styles. In addition, the extension activities can inspire tangents and detours for further investigations, celebrations of the living soil, and sustainable communities.

We encourage you to use this guidebook to paint a complete picture of the earthworm and its place in the world. May it inspire celebrations of the living soil and steps toward sustainable communities.

A Word About *Common Roots*
A Guide to An Integrated, Living Curriculum

Welcome to the Common Roots Guidebooks, a collection of hands-on seasonal projects and activities for the curious child.

The Common Roots Guidebooks have been designed for teachers, parents and community members to create a living curriculum for children which integrates the human and ecological roots of their own community. These K-6 Guidebooks offer hands-on learning activities and projects for children to discover the past, explore the present and build their common future. These adventures are developmentally designed along a 7-year journey that help tell the *story* of each child's community, from its very first inhabitants (grades K-2) to its local heritage (grades 3-4) to a look to the future (grades 5-6), thereby creating a living curriculum of meaningful activities.

These Guidebooks integrate traditional subjects into each of the projects and activities that build upon each other as the child moves from Kindergarten through Sixth Grade. **Social Studies** is an integral part of the historic theme gardens - the hub of the Common Roots learning process for each grade level. **The Applied Scientific Method** is part of every activity. Children marvel at fermentation processes as they bake bread; track the life cycle of seeds; observe the effects of weather, fertilizer, insects and worms in their own gardens; and investigate and analyze sources of local water for pollution. **Language arts** are acquired as children write garden journals, read recipes or create a community ecology-action newsletter. **Math skills** are developed through designing a garden, measuring cooking ingredients and graphing changes in ecosystems. **Art, music, dance** and **physical activity** are also integrated into the activities to allow children to celebrate seasons and the cultures they are learning about.

Common Roots is an *inquiry-based journey* for children, guided by their teachers and parents and accompanied by their elders and neighbors. The meaningful hands-on projects and activities nurture children's natural curiosity by providing the opportunity for each child to express their creativity and knowledge in order to answer their own questions. This student-centered approach engages students in the *process of learning* rather than providing textbook answers to rigid curriculums.

Common Roots provides children with real-life opportunities to develop problem solving skills to research, document and help preserve their fragile environ-

The Common Roots Journey

ment and disappearing heritage - building a better world for tomorrow. The projects and activities climax at the 6th Grade level, but the journey exploring our natural and human world is lifelong.

Put on your pack and come along with us!

Chapter 1

Welcome To The
Wonderful World Of Wigglers

Introducing...
The Amazing Earthworm!

Chapter 1

Welcome To The Wonderful World Of Wigglers

🐛 Why are these small, soil-loving creatures such a vital part of the web of life? What mysteries and curiosities do earthworms hold? What can we learn from these smooth-bodied animals of the dark underworld? Dive right in and explore with your students the wonderful, amazing, fascinating life of the earthworm!

Table of Contents   **Page**

Activity 1: The Wonder Of The Worm

Purpose:

This activity welcomes everyone to the world of earthworms, motivates curiosity and inquiry, and inspires appreciation for the simple miracle of the earthworm. A short puppet show introduces Wilma Worm and her family, followed by a close look at real worms. It is followed by an inquiry and a closing activity.

Materials:

> aluminum pie plates or styrofoam plates
> earthworms
> magnifying lenses
> paper and pencils
> several pieces of large paper (on a flip chart, if possible)
> giant pictures of the inside and the outside of the earthworm
>   (The sheets for this giant worm are in appendix.)
> Wilma Worm Puppet, "soil" (can be a brown bag or cloth)
> and plant for puppet show

Procedure:

1) For the **Wilma Worm Puppet Show,** children gather around the "soil" Earthworm Compost Farm, waiting quietly until Wilma pops up, seemingly from inside the bin. Wilma would like to introduce everyone to all her friends, cousins, aunts, uncles, children and grandchildren who will soon be living in the classroom Earthworm Compost Farm. All the earthworms are looking forward to making friends with their future caretakers. Wilma hopes that the students will be kind and gentle with the worms, for they are fragile beings that are easily squashed or harmed. (You might repeat this request for gentle handling, by reminding them to treat the earthworms with respect and care). In addition, she wants to convey what it is like to live in the soil, and why worms are so important to humans.

You may use the following dialogue if you wish, or make up your own.

Wilma Worm Puppet Show

"Hello, there, I am Wilma Worm. I would like to welcome all of you to the wonderful world of wigglers! We may seem like a squirmy bunch, but actually we are very hard workers and are a vital part of the web of life. Does anybody think they know why we are so marvelous?

"Ahem! Well, without us, you probably would not have food. You certainly would not be able to have a garden as the soil would not contain any of those important things you call **nutrients.** Does anybody know what a nutrient is? Nutrients help all living things grow. (Demonstrate a plant prop growing out of the bin.) A green plant becomes healthy and strong by using nutrients hidden in the soil. When the plant dies (plant can fall over), the nutrients are returned to the soil with the help of creatures like us. If you can believe it, we perform magic. We turn leaves and other plant matter, like the leftover food you eat, into rich, fertile soil, full of nutrients for your garden plants. Isn't that amazing?

"And as if that weren't enough, we **aerate** the soil, which means the holes we dig allow air to flow through the soil (very important for plants). Our holes also allow water to flow deeper into the ground. I must say, I *am* proud to be an earthworm!

"Let's take a trip into my world of soil and dark places. Find a place to get comfortable, lie down, and shut your eyes. This is not a time to giggle, but to relax, so that you can understand a little of what life is like for us.

"Imagine yourself under your garden, or under a forest floor. You live in deep, moist soil, slithering your way through tunnels you have dug. It is very dark in your home of earth, but that is how you like it. You feed at night under cover and safety of darkness. Your favorite foods are leaves and grass, but you love to eat leftover food whenever you can get it. Orange rinds, coffee grinds, lettuce leaves, apple cores - Yum!

"Feel yourself slithering, sliding, and crawling along through dark, earthy tunnels, squeezing up through the soil into the fresh night air. You crawl out onto the ground in search of tempting morsels to eat, like leaves, or perhaps you wish to go in search of a local compost pile.

"Let's all crawl like worms, looking for leaves. . . . Oh, how wonderful! What a find! Somebody raked a pile of leaves into a corner of the yard! Oak leaves, maple leaves, some cut grass, and oh, wow, what is this? A banana peel, your favorite! You crawl right onto the banana peel, which is sitting on top of the pile of leaves, and munch away in the moonlight. You can't stay out too long, because you need to keep moist so you can breathe through your skin. This warm night air isn't as bad as sunlight, which could dry you out very quickly.

"You must also be on the lookout for enemies - predators that might like to eat you! Oh, no! You feel the earth tremble - someone, or something is coming! Who is it? Is it only Otis, the dog, who is scared of his own shadow, or your friend Ratfink, the cat? Or is it something dangerous, like Molly Mole, Sheila Shrew? Or a bird, like Robin or Owl? Your five hearts seem to pound in your chest as you determine your next move.

"Crawl back to your hole as quickly as possible, for you know very well that Shrew, Mole, Owl or Robin would love to have you for dinner! Scrunch up and stretch out, scrunch and stretch, scrunch and stretch, as fast as you can. Thank goodness you recently grew a few more segments, for your segments have muscles that help you move. Crawl deeper into the leaves, faster now, into the moist, rich earth.

"Phew! You are now safely back in your home below the ground. Slowly, slowly your hearts - actually enlarged blood vessels - return to their normal beat. You will venture out again soon, when you are certain that danger is past, or when your hunger gets the better of you.

"Wasn't that fun, pretending to be a worm? Would you rather be a worm, instead of a human? You may all get up now and watch me again.

"Now that you have a sense of what it is like to be a worm, I would like to introduce you to all my friends, cousins, aunts, uncles, children and grandchildren who will soon be living in your classroom Earthworm Compost Farm. There are quite a few of us and soon there will be many, many more. You see, our population increases very fast. We double our numbers every month!

"Some names you will become familiar with include my cousins Mo and Joe. All of us are looking forward to making friends with you. We hope that you will be kind and gentle with us, for we are fragile beings who are easily squashed or harmed. We cannot tolerate being cut up, squashed, left out to dry, or drowned in water. So please, remember to treat us with respect and care. Thank you. Now I must slither back into my home of earth, where it is dark and moist. I will see you soon, so don't forget me!"

2) After Wilma crawls down into her home, children will certainly want to see some earthworms firsthand. Studying worms closely can be a real eye opener! Students can chose a buddy with whom to make some new worm friends.

The first time students meet the earthworms, let them observe and simply experience the earthworm as a whole being. Questions and observations can be recorded after this first meeting.

The worms can be handed out on pie plates with a clump of soil. Hand lenses greatly enhance what can be seen. Encourage students to touch the worms gently. (This might be a good time for a "treat worms with respect" reminder).

3) After students have had a chance to experience "earthworm essence", they may share their questions and observations with the rest of the class. The questions can be turned into research projects or experiments for class, small group, or self study. Posting these questions so that they are visible to everyone, and keeping a running list of questions as they come up, emphasizes the importance of this process and increases its success.

The following questions may be used to inspire students:

- What do you know about worms?
- Do you have any questions about worms?
- When and where have you seen worms?
- Do you think they are important? Why or why not?
- How does an earthworm move?

(continued)

- What do they do?
- Where do they live?
- What do they eat?
- Are there male and female worms?
- Does the worm have blood? A heart?
- How does the worm see in the dark?
- What do earthworms do when it gets cold?
- What eats earthworms?
- How do earthworms protect themselves?
- What do the earthworms do all day?
- Why are earthworms moist?
- Are earthworms all the same?
- Do worms have families?
- Can you find any babies?
- Can you tell which worms are the oldest? Can you find the youngest earthworm?
- How can you tell the difference between the adult and baby worms?
- How do earthworms move?

4) Let's all get up and do an earthworm dance! (The entire group can try to coordinate themselves to move like an undulating earthworm).

5) **Earthworm Caretakers** may suggest rules for taking care of worms.

This would be a good time to initiate a group discussion concerning respect and care of the earthworms. Following this discussion, your students might draw up an Earthworm Caretaker Agreement Contract, and have everyone sign it.

- How should we treat earthworms?
- What do you think the earthworms need?
- Why do you think the Earthworm Compost Farm has a black cover over it?
- What do you think earthworms eat?
- What kind of habitat do you think worms would like to be in?
- What can we do to keep the earthworms happy in their habitat?

6) The following ideas can be used for closure:

- Children may illustrate and label parts of the worm's exterior for their journals.
- Everyone can help write a group poem about the worm. Children can copy the poem and put it in their journal.
- Students can take turns sharing what they feel is special about a worm. They might like to illustrate this in their journals. (See Activity 2).

Activity Extension: Skin, Bones and Muscles

Children can compare their bodies to an earthworm's body.

- How does the earthworm's skin compare to our skin?
- Does an earthworm appear to have bones?
- How do we know we have bones in our body?
- How does an earthworm move?
- What do you think an earthworm uses to help it to move along?
- How do our muscles help us move our bodies?

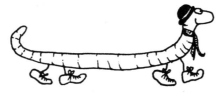

What's wrong with this picture?

Activity 2: My Earthworm Journal

Purpose:

The children may make journals that contain examples of their earthworm projects. The book can portray their scientific observations and experiments, poetry, illustrations, group projects and creative writing.

🐛 Encourage children to use their journals as a way to creatively express their learning. An interesting way for students to review and share their information as they experience the Wonderful World of Wigglers, is through drawing, painting, and writing stories or poetry.

Materials:

light cardboard for the cover	crayons
blank paper	watercolors
lined paper	markers

Procedure:

1) Children can design their own journals. They can make pockets to hold papers, or they can punch holes with a hole punch and hold the notebook together with string tied through the holes. They may also use rings from old notebooks to hold their journals together.

2) Each child can design his own cover page. Encourage students to take their time as they draw; this does not have to be a rushed product. The cover page can also be designed much later, after students have a real feel for the life of a worm and have made discoveries about worms.

Activity 3: Wormley's Believe It Or Not

Purpose:

Children can collect fascinating facts about earthworms.

Materials:

large paper for keeping a list of facts

Procedure:

1) Keep a running master list of facts in the classroom, accompanied by drawings. This list can be titled Wormley's Believe It Or Not. Children may also enjoy keeping their own illustrated lists in their journals.

2) What other interesting facts can the students think of? Could any of these facts inspire further research? Students can include the information they discover from their own research, based on questions they asked in the inquiry. In addition, as they discover fascinating worm trivia while moving through this earthworm journey, they can gradually add to *Wormley's Believe It Or Not.*

3) Use facts and trivia for a school-wide "What Am I? Earthworm Mystery Of The Week" contest. Or create a game patterned after T.V. game shows in which contestants answer questions about worms.

Some fascinating facts appear on the following page:

Wormley's Believe It Or Not

"I am one of the most important animals of the earth, yet few people realize how they depend on me. I am a recycler, humidifier, plower and air conditioner—all rolled into one! That means that I fertilize the soil with my droppings, and the holes I dig both aerate the soil and allow water to seep deeper into the ground. Without me, farmers would have a very hard time growing food. Many other animals would go hungry."

● One pound of earthworms (approximately 1,000 worms) will consume one pound of garbage in a day. In other words, a worm will eat the equivalent of its weight in one day.

● The earthworm population growth rate is phenomenal. 10 worms will double in one month. This number will increase to 640 worms in six months, become 10,240 worms in ten months, and eventually become 40,960 worms in a year! How many worms would you have in a year if you started with 1000 worms? If you started with 10 worms, how many worms would you have after 3 years?

● The earthworm has 50-200 segments. The segments are actually groups of muscles that the worm uses to crawl. These special muscles allow a worm to scrunch up and stretch out as it moves from one place to another.

● The earthworm has five hearts. These hearts are actually enlarged blood vessels that pump blood through the worm's body.

● Earthworms have both male and female parts. This is called **hermaphroditic**. They can lay 2 to 3 cocoons per week. These cocoons protect developing baby earthworms.

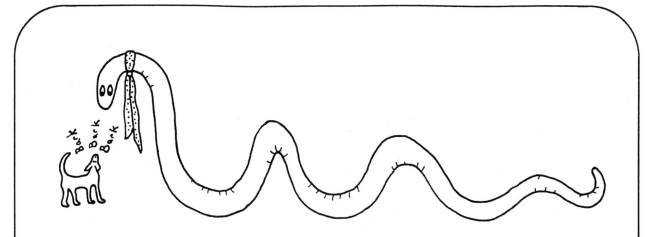

 The longest earthworm in the world measured 6.7 feet, found in South Africa!

 Earthworms can survive an hour or more under water!

 Earthworms have taste buds, and definite taste preferences!

 Cocoons can lie dormant in dry conditions, but will begin to develop and hatch baby worms if put into moist conditions.

Suggested References for Fact Collecting

Darling, Lois and Louis. *Worms,* William Morrow and Company, New York, NY, 1972.

McLaughlin, Mary. *Earthworms, Dirt and Rotten Leaves: An Exploration In Ecology,* Macmillan Publishing Company, New York, NY,1986.

Pigdon, Keith and Marilyn Woolley. *Earthworms,* Modern Curriculum Press, Cleveland, Ohio, 1989.

Simon, Seymour. *Discovering What Earthworms Do,* McGraw-Hill, New York, NY, 1969.

(continued)

Activity Extension: Earthworms Around the World

🐛 Research the different species of earthworms found around the world. This can be a journal exercise, or kids can display this research by plotting the species locations on a world map. The children can then surround the map with specie descriptions and illustrations.

Activity 4: Earthworm Anatomy Art

Purpose:

After carefully observing an earthworm's physical form, children reproduce a model of the earthworm using clay or other available materials.

Materials:

journals
pencils, markers, etc. for drawing
clay
materials for worm puppet

Procedure:

1) Hand out earthworms to pairs of children. In their journals, they can draw a detailed picture of the earthworm, which can be labeled with exterior anatomical parts. You can refer to the labeled illustration on page 84.

2) The children can then fashion a worm model from clay.

3) How could you construct a worm puppet large enough to fit several children inside? Brainstorm some ideas for creating a giant puppet with your students. (How about brown burlap attached to halved hula hoop segments that undulate like a real worm)?

Activity 5: Worms and Peace

Purpose:

This activity introduces the idea that worms can be a symbol or a metaphor for peace. We should treat all life with the same respect, care, and appreciation that we give the earthworms.

Materials:

art supplies for drawing or painting such as water colors, pastels, colored pencils, paper
examples of symbols
pictures that evoke peaceful feelings

Procedure:

1) One way to begin this activity is to initiate a discussion of symbols by asking children to define what a symbol is. Can they can give some specific examples? You might want to supplement some of their ideas with your own examples.

2) Invite the children to think of the different things a worm might symbolize. Ask them why they think worms might be a good symbol for peace. If we treat worms with gentleness and respect, isn't that a step towards peace? Shouldn't we treat *all* life with the same respect, care, and appreciation that we give the earthworms? Reverence for life evokes a peaceful state of mind, and can lessen the possibility of violence or harmful acts.

3) Challenge children to create a drawing or design using the earthworm as a symbol for peace.

Chapter 2

Building The Earthworm Compost Farm

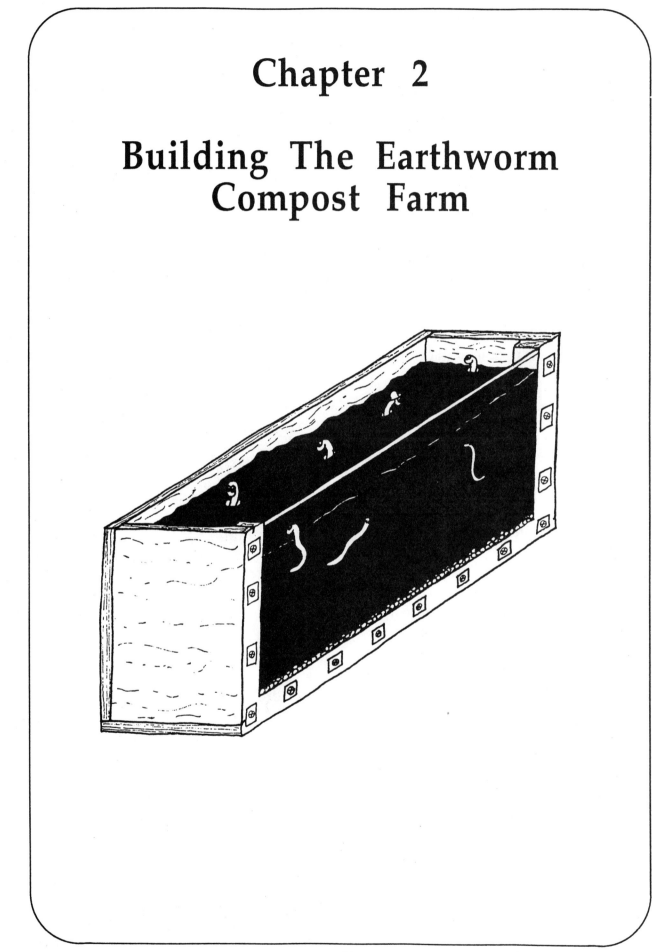

Chapter 2

Building the Earthworm Compost Farm

🐛 Children begin building the Earthworm Compost Farm with the help of parents and community members. The construction of the Farm is only part of this project. Researching the needs of the earthworms - food, light, bedding, moisture, temperatures - is also important. This information is included here, but students are encouraged to seek the information themselves by asking farmers, anglers, and elders who may have kept a worm farm in their childhood, or anyone else in the community who may have experience with raising worms. They can also use books in the library, but we emphasize human resources so children can meet other people who caretake earthworms.

Table Of Contents   Page

"The Big Move"

Edwina and Wally Earthworm were anxiously waiting for their father to come home. Their mother, Wilma, had told them he had some exciting news for them. What could it be? Were they going on vacation to the manure piles on Redworm Farm? Was he bringing home a special treat, like watermelon rind or a banana peel?

Soon they saw their father, Wilmur, crawling toward their front hole. They wriggled and wiggled in excitement, and crawled to greet him.

"What's the news, Dad?" asked Edwina.

Wilmur sat down on their front hole steps and sat his two excited wormlets down on his segments. He called to Wilma, who joined them in the cool shade of the early morning. "We are going to move to a new community, where we will live with lots of other worms in a classroom full of human children."

Edwina and Wally gasped in fear and surprise. They could not imagine anything more horrible than living near a bunch of human beings. From what they knew of human children, they would probably die within a week from being squashed, stomped on, drowned or cut in half.

Wilmur put up his hand to quiet their fear. "Now, I know just what you are thinking. But we are going to a special place. We are going to join some children who are learning to be Earthkeepers. The children know how to care for worms and look forward to making friends with you. They will not harm you, I promise. Your mother has met them, and says they will be very gentle and friendly. These children know that we worms are very important creatures who fertilize, aerate, and help water seep into the soil. The children want to show the world how magnificent we are, and to tell everyone that one path towards a peaceful world is to understand and respect all living things, no matter how big or how small."

"But - but where will we live? What will it be like?" asked a worried Wally.

"Ah, it will be paradise!" promised Wilma. "We will be living in a bin, or on an Earthworm Compost Farm as the children call it. The soil will be moist, so you can breathe easily through your skin. The temperature will be an ideal 55-77 degrees F. Plenty of gourmet food. Lots of soft peat moss and vermiculite to crawl around in. And a dark blanket to keep out the light."

Edwina and Wally just about wiggled out of their father's lap, they were so excited! They could not wait to begin the adventure that lay ahead.

Activity 1: Building the Earthworm Compost Farm

Purpose:

Building the Earthworm Compost Farm is a wonderful opportunity to involve parents and community members in the children's experience. Local farmers and gardeners may be interested in visiting the group to share their experiences with earthworms.

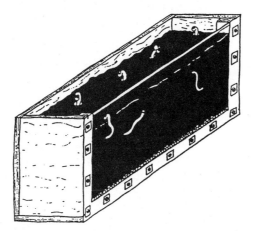

🐛 This bin is designed as an Earthworm Compost Farm composting system. It can be built for $35.00 using new materials. The bin can also be made from an old wooden box, or a variety of recycled materials. All Earthworm Compost Farms must have a porous bottom to allow for drainage.

🐛 You can try to find earthworms (red wigglers) locally, or they may be ordered from the following sources:
* Flower Field Enterprises, 10332 Shaver Road, Kalamazoo, MI 49002
    telephone 616-327-0108.
* B & P, Box 398, Olathe, CO 81425
* Cape Cod Worm Farm, 30 Center Ave, Buzzards Bay, MA 02532

Materials:

3/4" plywood cut to the following dimensions:
      side A - 8" x 12"
      side B - 8" x 12"
      bottom - 8 3/4" x 24"
      back - 12" x 24"

1" x 2" boards cut to the following dimensions (for front of bin):
      side A - 12"
      side B - 12"
      bottom edge - 21"

1 12 3/4" x 24" piece of clear plexiglass
30 wood screws
12 1" wood screws
rubber strip, cut into 1" squares
silicone sealant
screening
strong rope
pebbles
black felt
staples
circular saw
drill
staple gun
scissors

Procedure:

1) Order plexiglass - hardware stores will often cut pieces for you.

2) Cut sides, back and bottom to dimensions shown above.

(continued)

3) Screw back and sides together, so that the side panels are in the inside of the back panel.

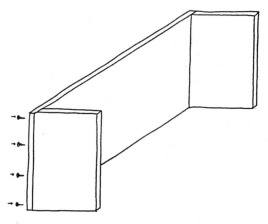

4) Screw bottom onto sides and back, making sure all edges are even.

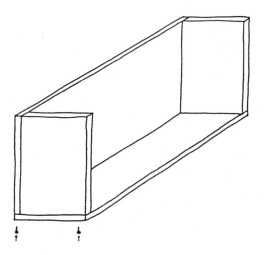

5) Screw in the 12" pieces of 1" x 2" to the inside edges of the front.

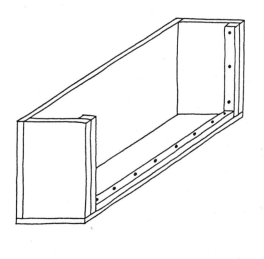

6) Slip in the 21" piece of 1" x 2" in between the 12" pieces, so it is flush with the front edge and bottom.

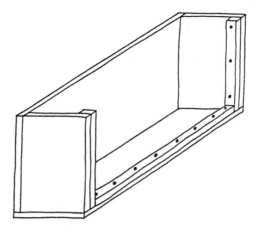

7) Squeeze a thin film of silicone onto the front face.

8) Pierce squares of rubber with wood screws.

9) Carefully drill plexiglass to front of bin using 1" wood screws. The rubber gaskets should be placed between the plexiglass and each screw.

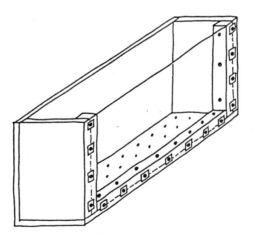

10) Drill approximately 12 1/8" holes in the bottom for drainage. Staple the screening over the holes. Now you are ready to put the worms to bed!

Earthworms in Paradise

For a happy, healthy earthworm community, follow these suggestions about bedding, food, temperature, light and ventilation.

Bedding

     Worms will thrive in a number of different bedding materials, but for classroom use we recommend a combination of peat moss and vermiculite. These are inexpensive and widely available at farm and garden centers, as well as at most hardware stores.

     To prepare the bedding, mix about 3 pounds of peat moss with 4 cups of vermiculite in a large container. Next, add a gallon plus 2 cups of water and mix well. Place the mixture in the worm bin, taking care not to compress it.

     Now you may put the earthworms into their new home! You can celebrate with an earthworm housewarming party! Feed them vegetable scraps and coffee grounds.

> **Note:** Bedding must be changed every six months or it becomes toxic to the worms. The procedure for this is outlined at the end of this chapter.

Moisture

     Since a worm's body is 75%-90% water, it is important to remember to keep the worm bedding moist. Moreover, worms need to be wet to breathe. They breathe through their skin, and if their bedding is not moist enough they will suffocate. You should be able to squeeze a handful of the bedding into a ball, so that it holds its shape. If the mixture crumbles, then you need to add more water. If water drips out of the ball when you squeeze it, or if the worms are crawling out of the bin, the soil is too wet. In the latter case, add more dry material.

Temperature

     Keep the temperature between 55 and 75 degrees F. If the

temperature falls too much below this range, the worms will stop repro-
ducing. Temperatures greater than 84 degrees F can be fatal to the
worms.

Light

❧ Worms are sensitive to light, and therefore will hide inside the
bedding unless a black cloth is placed over the bin. Keep the bin away
from sunlight. Pull off the cloth and watch the worms slip down into
the soil!

Feeding

❧ Since there is no food present in peat, the worms will need to
be fed regularly. Worms can eat just about any kind of vegetable scraps,
but they do **not** like meat or cheese products. Refer to the accompany-
ing food list for worm food ideas. In general, chop the food finely and
disperse it evenly beneath the surface.

❧ After a few months, the classroom bin should be able to
handle up to two pounds of food per week, which is about 1/3 lb. of
food a day. This may vary in different conditions, and it may take
awhile for the worm population to increase enough so it can handle this
much food. For the first month or two, experiment with how much food
the earthworms will eat. Don't put in more food until the old food is at
least partially decomposed. To prevent problems with fruit flies, always
bury the food by covering it with bedding.

Creative Endeavors to Embellish the Bin

❧ Cover the top of the soil of the Earthworm Compost Farm
with leaves, moss, shelf fungus, bark, and other items to make it seem
more homey for the worms.

❧ The black felt covering for the Earthworm Compost Farm can
be decorated with colorful, hand-made wiggly worms. Use different
materials, and stitch or glue them on to the cover.

Gourmet Food for Earthworms

Earthworms are fond of the following foods:

banana peels
orange rinds
apples
bread crusts
eggs
egg shells
carrots
celery
beans
potatoes
tomatoes
cucumbers
grapefruit rinds
lettuce
onion peel
pears
coffee grounds
tea leaves
cabbage
corn bread
cereal
pancakes
waffles
kale
broccoli

Earthworms in Paradise Daily Observation Sheet

1) Is the soil too dry? Check by squeezing a clump of bedding in your hand. If it sticks together in a ball, it's fine. If the ball falls apart, then you need to add water.

2) Is the soil too wet? Are the worms crawling out of the bin? Can you squeeze drops of water out of a clump of bedding? Don't add water! Add some dry material, such as peat moss.

3) Do the earthworms have enough food? Has the food partly or mostly disappeared? If much of the food is still there, the earthworms probably have enough to eat.

4) What is the temperature of the soil? It should be between 55 and 77 degrees F. If the soil temperature is out of this range, move the bin to a cooler or warmer spot.

5) Did you mix up the soil from the bottom of the bin to allow air to circulate?

6) Where are most of the worms? Are they gathering in one place, or are they scattered evenly throughout the bin?

7) Take a clump of soil from the middle of the bin and **look for cocoons.** They look like apple seeds, but are a little smaller. Cocoons vary in color from cream to dark red, getting darker as they mature. If you are very lucky and have sharp eyes, you might even be able to watch some baby worms hatch from the cocoon!

8) Use the Daily Observation Sheet provided on the next page to chart the progress of your Earthworm Compost Farm.

LIFE WITH EARTHWORMS: DAILY OBSERVATION SHEET

Date	Number of worms you see	Any eggs?	Food (Describe)	Check moisture

Activity 2: Community Opportunities

Purpose:

To provide opportunities for parent and community involvement.

Procedure:

Some ideas include:

- **Field trips** and **interviews** of farmers or individuals raising earthworms.

- **Meeting** a soil conservationist, ice fisherpeople who raise earthworms, people who raise and sell night crawlers, and home composters.

🐛 Human resources give the children an opportunity to experience the significance of earthworms outside of the classroom, in a broader context. These contacts can also provide opportunities for apprenticeships. Apprenticeships are a wonderful way to develop working relationships with adults who are directly involved with earthworms. These community members can be a source of inspiration as well as role models for caretaking earthworms.

🐛 The following are examples of Community Service Projects and Entrepreneurial Opportunities for class community building. A coordinated parent/school/community program can create a framework for the children to present their projects and products - as well as workshops - to the community.

- **Raise and sell earthworms** for gardening and fishing.

- Sell vermicompost (fertile soil made by earthworms) at a **Community Soil Celebration** in the Spring. You can separate the earthworms from the soil or sell the soil with the earthworms.

- Children may lead indoor **Earthworm Compost Farm workshops** for recycling kitchen garbage in Winter for the school, parents and community.

• Children and community volunteers may construct and sell **Indoor Earthworm Compost Farm Kits** which may include an Earthworm Compost Farm, starter worms and an informative instruction booklet written by students.

Activity Extensions:

A Day In the Life of An Earthworm Compost Farm

🐛 Children can make daily observations of the Earthworm Compost Farm by using the Daily Observation sheet.

Down On the Earthworm Compost Farm

🐛 Children can interview elders and other community members who might have used, or are currently using, earthworms to recycle their food scraps.

Earthworm Nutrition

🐛 Refer to the sheet "Gourmet Food For Earthworms" (pg.40)
  • What food groups do earthworms eat from?
  • What food groups do they not eat from?
  • How does their diet compare to ours?
    - Make a list of foods that earthworms eat that we don't, such as oak leaves.
    - Make another list of foods that they don't eat that we do, such as cheese.
  • Children can compare their diets with the earthworms' diet.

Activity 3: Math, Nature's Way: Good Bye Garbage!

Purpose:

In this activity, children determine how many pounds of worms are needed to recycle the food waste generated by their family or group. This process helps determine whether the worms have enough food, or if there are enough worms to consume the food waste.

Note: The math problems in this activity are based on a bin 6 feet square, a size that allows for a large amount of food waste to be recycled. If your bin is large enough, all you need to worry about is the number of worms. The ratio of worms to garbage (in pounds) is 2/1. Thus, for every 2 lbs of worms, you can recycle 1 lb of garbage per week.

Materials:

> scale for weighing food scraps
> rulers to measure dimensions of earthworm bin
> pencils
> paper
> calculator (optional)

Procedure:

1) First, calculate the average amount of food waste (in pounds) that your family/class generates each week. (Keeping track of the food waste over several weeks will ensure a more accurate average.)

2) Once you have calculated this average, divide it by 7 to obtain the average amount of food waste in pounds your family/class generates per day.

(continued)

3) Now figure the number of pounds of worms you need, based on the 2/1 worm-to-garbage ratio.

Activity Extension

🐛 Challenge the children to consider how worm composting at home, school, or in the community might impact the landfill problems society faces.

- How much room does 2 pounds of food waste take up?
- How much space does three weeks of food waste take up?
- How much vermicompost (soil made by worms) is made by worms in two months?
- Are there worms in landfills?
- Visit a landfill.

Example

🐛 A class weighed its weekly food leftovers for a month, and got the following results: 2 lbs, 3 lbs, 5 lbs, 4 lbs.

- How much total food waste did they generate? 14 lbs.
- What is the weekly average? 3.5 lbs.
- What is the daily average? 1/2 lb.
- How many pounds of worms do they need? 1 lb.

🐛 Calculate the total waste, weekly average, daily average, and pounds of worms needed in the following situations.

1) Weekly figures of 5 lbs, 5 lbs, 7 lbs , 3 lbs.
2) Weekly figures of 3 lbs, 4 lbs, 3 lbs, 2 lbs.
3) 15 pounds of leftovers for four weeks.
4) 20 pounds of leftovers for five weeks.
5) 12 pounds of leftovers for three weeks.

Activity 4: Soil Tests

Purpose:

Children may conduct soil tests to determine whether the nutritional content of the soil in the Earthworm Compost Farm changes over time.

Discovery Question:

Will the nutritional content of the soil in the Earthworm Compost Farm change over time?

Materials:

soil test kit
wall chart to keep track of the results

Procedure:

1) Purchase a soil test kit from your local hardware store or garden center.

2) Discuss with children the effect earthworms might have on soil. What questions do students have? The following questions may supplement theirs and initiate discussion.

- How do earthworms help the soil?
- How do you think earthworms help plants?
- How do you think humans benefit from earthworms?
- What do you think would happen to the soil if there were no earthworms?

3) Explain to your students that they will be conducting soil tests to see if the soil in the Earthworm Compost Farm changes over time. They will be testing for 3 nutrients (Nitrogen, Potassium, Phosphorous) and acidity (pH). Nutrients in the soil feed plants. We depend on the nutrients in plants to help us grow and stay healthy and strong. **Optional:** Students may research the function of Nitrogen, Potassium, and Phosphorous in human diets.

4) Show students how to use the test kit. They can take turns testing the soil in the Earthworm Compost Farm, which should be done every 2 - 3 weeks. Keep a wall chart of test results near the Earthworm Compost Farm.

5) After several months, discuss the results. The nutrient content of the soil, as well as the acidity, should increase. An earthworm's casting is full of nutrients that were previously locked up in the plant. In the process of digesting organic material, earthworms make nutrients available again for plants and, ultimately, humans.

Chapter 3

Earthworms In Action

I'm a recycler, humidifier, plower and air conditioner all rolled into one!

Chapter 3

Earthworms In Action

Once the earthworms are safely settled in their home, children can begin investigating the work of the worm. This should include the worms' role in the soil ecosystem and their effect on the indoor garden. This section, *Earthworms In Action,* contains investigations that should reflect the students' interests. The objective of these experiments lies in the *process* children must undergo to seek an answer. Students can then go on to devise their own experiments, using the questions they came up with during the inquiry.

Table Of Contents   **Page**

Introduction to the Experimental Method

Experiments allow us to explore questions about the world. You can begin by asking: **What will happen if...?** You then make **predictions** about what you think will happen. Next you follow a **procedure,** or a set of directions. As the experiment progresses, **observe** and **record what happens,** and then make **conclusions** based on what you learned.

Here are some things to consider when designing an experiment:

🐛 Begin by defining or describing what you want to find out and why.

🐛 Choose one *variable* that will be different, and keep all other variables constant. Variables are all the different things that might have an effect on the experiment, such as light, temperature, moisture, oxygen, or materials used in the experiment.

🐛 Always have a *control* group in your experiment. A control group is exposed to the normal conditions, whereas the *test* groups will be exposed to the variables.

🐛 Repeat the experiment or run at least two sets of the experiment at the same time. This helps to prevent possible errors in your procedure.

🐛 Decide what to observe. What are you looking for? How often will you be making observations/measurements? How will you organize the information (*data*) you gather? Charts and graphs are good ways to put together the data you have collected.

🐛 In making conclusions, you will be tying together the data you have collected and seeing if you have answered the questions you originally raised. You may also discover some unexpected results. This could lead to more questions and experiments.

🐛 The following *Discovery Sheet* may be used by children who wish to design their own experiments based on their interests and questions from the inquiry.

Explorations and Experiments

My Discovery question: What will happen if . . . ?

My Prediction: What I think will happen is . . . .

My Data: (Observations/Measurements) What happened was . . . .

My Conclusion: I learned that . . . .

Activity 1: The Great Transformation

Purpose:

This experiment will allow children to see how earthworms mix up the soil as they move through it and transform plant matter into rich soil. Children may enjoy working in pairs, using the Explorations and Experiments student discovery sheet.

Discovery Question:

What will happen to the layers of soil in a jar if we add earth worms to it?

Prediction:

Children guess what they think will happen.

Materials:

> two glass containers the same size for each small group or pair of students
> soil samples: clay, sand, garden soil, humus, leaves - enough to fill jars
> journals

The following story might be a fun way to introduce the experiment.

"Close Encounters of the Worm Kind"

Mo and Joe earthworm were happily munching on some maple leaves that had fallen into the garden during a recent windstorm. It was a warm, soft summer night with a full moon - perfect for dining out. Occasionally they stopped and chatted with several other garden visitors, including Gomez the Groundhog and a pair of deer that were hoping to find some tender bean seedlings.

Suddenly, the family that owned the garden let out their dog, Otis, for an evening airing. Otis, who was pampered and well-loved, felt it was his duty to be a garden watch dog. He ran out to the garden and barked his most ferocious bark, which was actually a rather wimpy bark. None the less, Gomez and the deer scampered away to the woods, where they knew they were safe.

Otis, proud of himself for scaring away the garden pests, wandered over to the edge of the garden where he thought he had hidden his bone. Snuffling through the leaves, he came upon Mo and Joe, who were not afraid of Otis. They were still munching on maple leaves.

Otis, however, was startled. He had never met a worm in his life and, being the garden guard dog, was instantly suspicious of the two segmented, dark red characters that were calmly dining in the moonlight.

"WHO ARE YOU?" asked Otis in what he thought was a threatening tone of voice. "And what are you doing in my garden?"

"Hey, cool it, Otis, ol' boy. We help your garden. We actually fertilize the garden so plants can grow big and strong."

Otis, a little upset that these little critters did not seem to be the least bit afraid of him, and very surprised that they knew his name, tried to keep his tough attitude.

"Oh yeah? Prove it!"

Mo and Joe slithered right up onto the dog's nose. "Take us to your family!" chorused the worms. Otis looked at them in cross-eyed disbelief. He did not like the feel of the slimy creatures on his nose at all, and ran inside to show his family. He felt a little silly with Mo and Joe sitting right between his eyes, but his family was delighted.

"Oh, look what Otis brought us!" exclaimed Mrs. Rumpus.

"Oh yeah, a worm! Eat it, Otis!" encouraged the son, Rudolph.

"No, no!" said Mrs. Rumpus. "Worms are very important creatures. We must let them live."

"Why are they so important? What do they do?" demanded Regina, Rudolph's twin sister.

"Well, let's keep them as pets and find out!" suggested Ronald, the father. "I know Mrs. Annelid is keeping a worm bin in her class, and her students are learning all kinds of interesting things about earthworms."

"Yeah, I'll bet that's where Edwina, Wally and their parents are," said Mo to Joe. "They made it sound like it was a pretty nice place they were going to. Maybe we'll get fed gourmet food!"

The following is a description of the experiment that the Rumpus family designed to discover what earthworms do.

Procedure:

1) Obtain two glass containers the same size (wide-mouth gallon jars are ideal for this).

2) In both containers, children layer from bottom to top an inch or two of each of the following: clay, sand, soil, humus, leaves. Label one container A, and the other B.

3) Ask the children to draw pictures of each container. At this point, both should look quite similar.

4) When children finish drawing, they may carefully place worms into container A, the **variable**. Feed the worms kitchen scraps or leaves. Add water to moisten the soil because worms need a moist environment. Make sure the soil stays moist! Add water, leaves and kitchen scraps to container B as well. This container will be your **control**. Cover each jar with black cloth or paper.

5) Each day, children can remove the coverings and observe any changes.

What do they see? Can they find any tunnels? What other evidence can they find of earthworms doing their work? They can describe their observations in words or drawings.

6) After two weeks, discuss the changes students have seen. How is the earthworm like a plow? How do the tunnels help the soil? How does the earthworm help recycle plant matter? What would happen if there were no earthworms to recycle food scraps? What is happening in the container that has no worms? How is jar A different from jar B?

7) Return the earthworms to the Earthworm Compost Farm, and watch them burrow back into their home.

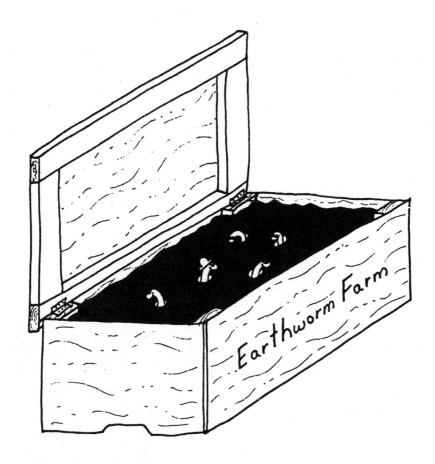

"In Search of Adventure"
A Guided Journey

    🐛 *After the experiment, you might want to read the following guided journey to the children. Encourage them to shut their eyes and put their heads down, or have them lie down on the floor. This may help them to relax and focus on the imagery.*

Imagine you are an earthworm, slithering through sun-warmed soil. You have been living in this particular patch of soil beneath a tree for some time, and are quite well acquainted with the roots, mushrooms, ants, fellow earthworms and other neighbors.

"Recently you have been itchy to go on an adventure. You are getting tired of the same old diet of grass and leaves, and a lot of your good friends have gone away. Yesterday, you overheard a new neighbor, Edward Earthworm the Second, speak of places and things beyond your wildest imagination! It sounded so exciting that you've decided to leave first thing tomorrow night, under cover of darkness, when it is safe for earthworms to move about.

"And now it is night, a few hours after sunset. A thin sliver of moon hangs in the western sky, and stars twinkle in the clear night. You breathe the cool night air through your skin and excitedly slip out of your home. As you crawl over the ground you wonder what adventures you will encounter, who you might meet, and what soils are out there.

"You begin by tunneling along under the edge of the garden. You crawl under rocks and between roots, occasionally meeting up with other soil friends, such as mushrooms and mites. Soon you decide it is safe enough to go up onto the ground. You feel yourself crawling over dry leaves and sticks. It's kind of scratchy and crinkly, but it smells nice, like decaying leaves. It's kind of fun to crawl up and over or under all the leaves and around the sticks. You guess, from what Edward said, that you have entered the Great Woods.

"Suddenly you bump into something cold and hard, with sharp, rough edges. You try to take a bite but find it impossible. 'Oh, this must be a rock! I wonder what it would be like to climb this?' You slither up the rock into a soft, moist bed of moss. And sure enough, some yummy oak leaves lie right in front of you. You stop for a snack, and then continue on your way.

"After a long time, you begin to tire and think about taking a rest. You burrow down through the scratchy, crinkly leaves and start to make a tunnel into the soil. You feel tired and crabby, and simply can't wait to put your head down in a soft bed of soil.

"But, wait, what is this? This isn't the nice, soft soil of home that gives easily as you plow through it. This is really tough stuff!

" 'ENNERRGGGHH! This is hard to move through! And Yuk! It tastes terrible! What have you gotten yourself into? Oh no, it must be that dreaded clay stuff . . . .'

"You stop to think for a minute. What will happen to you? Will you be able to find a safe place to sleep? And what other adventures will you encounter?"

Children may like to finish this story on their own, and then share it with the class. They can write and illustrate their endings in their journals, and/or create a play or puppet show about the earthworm's adventures. What would it be like to move through a landfill, sand, a desert, a marsh, or over a mountain?

Activity 2: The Mystery of the Puddled Earthworm

Purpose:

Children will see that too much water can be harmful to worms, because water fills up their burrows. At the same time, earthworm tunnels are an important way for water to percolate deeper into the soil.

Materials:

Shoe box
earthworms
soil
water

Procedure:

1) Have children form into small cooperative groups. Each child should choose one of the following roles: observer, task watcher, time keeper, note taker, speaker.

2) Take a walk with your students after a heavy rainfall. Challenge them to be detectives: to find as many clues as they can to prove it recently rained. Encourage them to observe, listen, and look for all the changes a rain can bring.

3) If students find several earthworms, the following questions can be used to stimulate discussion:

- Did they find any earthworms on the ground, in puddles, or on the pavement? Are they alive?

- What are the possible causes of death? Could they have drowned? Could exposure to light be harmful to them?

(continued)

4) The following experiment demonstrates what happens to worms during a heavy rainstorm. Place earthworms and soil into a shoe box . After several days, put the box in a sink and slowly pour room temperature water into the box until you notice something happening.

What happens? Why do the worms emerge from the soil into the light when usually they shy away from it?

As soon as possible after this observation, put the worms back into their real home.

5) Discuss with children the relationship between earthworms, soil, and rain. The earthworms dig tunnels that help water seep deeper into the soil. But if too much rain falls, the earthworms' holes fill up and they may drown. Soft, gentle rains allow the worms to burrow to safety.

Activity 3: Do Earthworms Like Deserts?

Purpose:

Children explore the earthworms' tendency to be drawn to moisture.

Discovery Question:

What will happen if we place worms in a container in which one side is dry and the other side is moist?

Materials:

>   small aquarium tank
>   cardboard
>   moist soil
>   water
>   20 earthworms

Procedure:

🐛 This experiment is done as a demonstration, but children can be involved in setting up the materials.

1) Students should place several inches of soil into the bottom of the tank. Next, place cardboard in the middle of the tank as a divider. Push the cardboard divider an inch or two down into the soil.

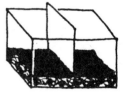

2) Now students can add more soil on both sides of the divider. They can scatter the worms on the surface of the soil, making sure they deposit the same number of worms on each side . The sides of the tank should be labeled A and B.

3) Students should water both sides of the tank well, so that the soil is moist enough. *(Soil moisture test: squeeze a handful; if it holds its shape, but does not drip water, then it's just right!)* Side B should dry out, but students need to remember to keep side A moist. Remind them to feed the worms on both sides!

4) After a week or so, choose one or two students to gently dig up the soil on both sides and count the worms. Which side has the most worms? Why?

Results and Conclusion:

Children can record their discovery questions, their predictions, observations and conclusions in their journals. Or they may use the "Explorations and Experiments" student discovery sheet to write up the investigation.

Activity 4: The Squirmy Worm

Purpose:

In this activity, children creatively express what they have been learning in their study of earthworms.

Materials:

> pencils
> paper
> water colors
> colored pencils
> crayons

Procedure:

1) Based on their observation, children may write a descriptive, creative poem about earthworms. The final copy may be written on a watercolor wash painting and entered in their Worm Journals.

2) In addition, children might like to make a collection of illustrated worm poetry and earthworm facts, which they can then publish and sell. These booklets could be distributed to the school library, public library, or local coffee shops, garden centers, or restaurants.

Activity 5: Dancing With Worms

Purpose:

Children can act out worm movements.

Materials:

Optional: musical instruments, or music on tape.

Procedure:

1) After watching how the worms move, let each child try to move like a worm. Encourage the student to imagine being a worm.

2) Students might like to imitate worm movements to different kinds of music.

3) The children can line up and hold each other's shoulders. Challenge them to imitate the expansion/contraction mode of worm movement. How many different ways can the group imitate the worm's movement?

4) How might the worm react to danger? To food placed near it? To light and darkness? Each student can act out a different response.

Activity 6: An Earthworm Garden

Purpose:

> *Do earthworms affect plant growth?*

> **Note:** This activity takes 6-8 weeks to complete.

Discovery Question:

> How do earthworms affect plant growth?

Materials:

> Indoor garden, or grow lights set up over plants
> vermicompost from Earthworm Compost Farm
> potting soil
> containers for plants (pint-sized milk cartons work fine)
> bean seeds
> Experimental Method Discovery Sheet (at end of activity)
> graph paper

Procedure:

> **Note:** If there is not an indoor garden or grow lab in your classroom, you may either set up grow lights over the containers, or place plants in a sunny window.

1) Using a cardboard divider, set aside an area of the indoor garden. You may wish to title this section "Experiments in Progress". Divide this experiment station in half, labeling one half **A - vermicompost**, and the other, **B - sterile potting soil**. You can also use containers to separate the two variables.

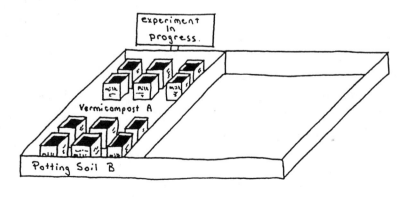

🐛 Children can organize themselves into two groups representing the two different kinds of soils. Encourage each to come up with a name for its group. Students may also work in groups of two, each pair having its own experiment.

🐛 Children can use the *"Experimental Method Discovery Sheet"* to write up their experiments. You might encourage them to help each other fill out the questions.

2) In the vermicompost section "A", fill recycled pint-sized milk cartons with vermicompost soil from the Earthworm Compost Farm. In the potting soil "B" section, fill milk cartons with potting soil.

3) Plant 2-3 bean seeds in each milk carton. As the bean seedlings emerge, thin them to one per carton.

4) Both sections should be exposed to the same light, water, and temperature conditions. Students can record the average light exposure (by recording the number of hours of light the plants receive), average temperature, and amount of water in their earthworm journals. A master record should be kept near the indoor garden.

5) Place a sheet of graph paper behind the plants to chart their growth. This will give students a consistent method to compare the growth rate of plants in the different soils. In addition to comparing growth rate, students should be looking for differences in plant

health by carefully observing the leaves. Yellowed or curled leaves indicate the soil is lacking in nutrients.

a) Ask students to make predictions. What do they think will happen to the plants in each section? Will there be any difference in growth rate between the plants growing in the different soils? Will the soils affect the health of the plants?

Results:

The children should observe and record information daily for a period of six weeks. They will be comparing the height, health, and any other observable differences between plants. In addition, students may wish to graph their records of light, temperature, water and plant growth.

> *Note:* The bean plants should reach maturity in eight to ten weeks. Students can then count the number of beans per plant to see if the soils affect seed production.

Conclusion:

What do students think produced the observed results?

Activity Extensions:

🐛 **Vermicompost Fertilizer:** What might happen if **house plants** are fed vermicompost on a regular basis? The growth and health of vermicompost-fed plants can be compared with plants that do not receive this feeding. Spider plants, ivy, philodendron, and coleus are low-light plants that are easy to grow. Feed plants by sprinkling a handful of vermicompost around the base of the plants.

🐛 Children might also wish to try raising **flowering plants**. (Geraniums are easy to grow.) Flowering is often an indicator of a healthy, well fed plant. As above, one set of plants should receive feeding with vermicompost, and the other set no such feeding. Run this experiment for a month. Students should keep daily records and compare results.

(continued)

🐛 Try making **vermicompost tea**! Add 4 parts water to 1 part vermicompost, shake well, and let stand in a warm, sunny window for a week.

What would happen if we fed this tea to plants in the indoor garden? Immediately before feeding the plants, shake the container of vermicompost tea again, then water the plants. Try an experiment comparing the effectiveness of vermicompost tea. Water some plants with the tea and others with tap water. What differences, if any, appear over the period of a month?

An Earthworm Garden

Date	Height		Number of Leaves	Color of Leaves	Other Notes
	A				
	B				
	A				
	B				
	A				
	B				
	A				
	B				

Chapter 4

Inside, Outside, Upside Down

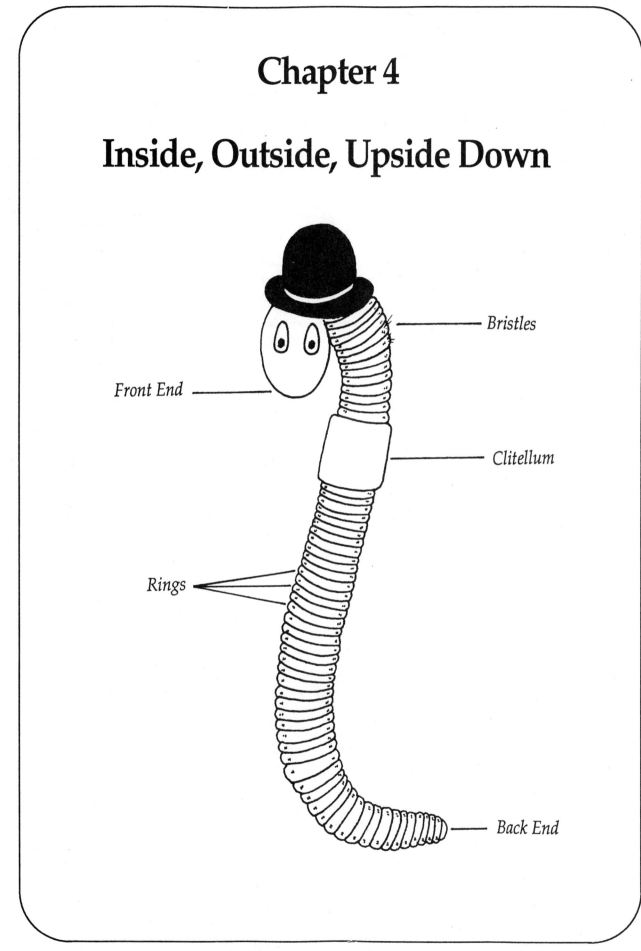

Bristles

Front End

Clitellum

Rings

Back End

Chapter 4

Inside, Outside, Upside Down

In this chapter, students take a closer look at the interior and exterior of the earthworm. They can make detailed observations of its outside anatomy and explore the secrets of the earthworm's insides. They can also investigate the earthworm's responses to its environment, including light and sound.

> **Note**: The investigations included throughout the rest of the guide range in difficulty from gentle observations to more sophisticated experiments for the gifted or motivated learner. As an alternative to class investigations, these activities are designed with a student-directed approach, allowing students to work at their own pace. In addition, students may be encouraged to design their own experiments based on their interest and their questions from the inquiry process.

Table Of Contents   Page

Activity 1: Does A Worm Wear Rings, and Does it Really Have Whiskers?

Purpose:

This activity gives the children a chance to observe the earthworm closely, and to begin to explore its form and function.

Discovery Question:

What can we learn from observing an earthworm closely?

Materials:

2 earthworms for each group of two children
1 hand lens for each child
1 plate
water
earthworm anatomy sheets

Optional: *Earthworms,* by Kieth Pigdon and Marilyn Woolly, a beautifully illustrated, large print book, 22" x 17", available from Modern Curriculum Press, 3900 Prospect Rd., Cleveland, Ohio, 44136.

Procedure:

1) Each pair of children should place a thin film of water (about 1/4 cup) on their plates. This will give the earthworms a moist surface on which to rest while being observed. Pass out the earthworm anatomy sheets. These can be filled in as you ask the questions below.

2) Bring out the worms and place one or two on each plate. Ask students to restate how they should handle earthworms.

3) Have students observe the **segments**, or rings on the worms. How many segments does each worm have? Whose worm has the most rings?

4) Ask students to find the swollen region on the earthworm. This is called the **clitellum.** It is where eggs, or cocoons, form. It is also called the band or girdle. Students can explore this in more detail in the next chapter.

5) How long is each worm? Children can estimate, then measure the length of their worms. Whose worm is the longest? Whose worm is the shortest? Each worm has a specific length. What is the average length? Does length have anything to do with age?

6) Students can pick up the earthworm and observe its soft, moist body. Do students think there are any bones in the earthworm?

7) Is the earthworm's body perfectly smooth? Using the hand lens, challenge students to find the **bristles** (like tiny whiskers) on the worm's body. What do they think the bristles are used for? Encourage them to hold the earthworm gently and stroke it. Can they feel the tiny bristles?

🐛 The worm uses bristles for protection. Has anyone ever seen a robin try to pull an earthworm out of the soil? (A worm does not simply slip out of the soil; it hangs on for dear life with its bristles!).

🐛 Bristles also aid the earthworm in crawling. First, it anchors itself with the rear bristles and stretches forward. Then, it holds on with the front bristles and moves the rear of its body forward.

8) How do students think an earthworm moves through the soil? What parts of its body do students think an earthworm uses to make tunnels?

9) Can the children figure out which end is the earthworm's head? Which end is the rear? Is there any reason to avoid the rear end of the worm and its function? What is special about the worm's scat, or **castings?**

10) Can an earthworm tell which end is up? What will happen if an earthworm is turned on its back? (*Note: As this is a beginning activity, demonstrate this for the children. It is an excellent way to model gentleness and respect for the earthworm.*)

11) Does an earthworm have eyes, or ears? Can an earthworm really see? Can it hear?

12) Can students find an earthworm's mouth? How does an earthworm see if it has no eyes? How does an earthworm breathe if it has no nose? To discover how an earthworm eats, sees, and breathes, move on to the next section . . . .

Sense Organs

🐛 Earthworms do not see or hear the way we do. They do not have ears or eyes, but they are sensitive to light and noise.

🐛 An earthworm hears by feeling vibrations. If you have a drum, let the children take turns placing their hand on the skin of the drum, feeling the vibration when the drum is struck. As another example, have one child lie down on the floor, covering his/her ears. As another child walks by, the child on the floor should be able to feel the vibrations of the footsteps. This is how a worm hears.

🐛 Earthworms are sensitive to vibrations transmitted through the earth. Moles digging through the earth usually cause the earthworm to leave its burrow. Wood turtles stomp the ground in a way that causes earthworms to come out of the soil. The turtles promptly eat the emerging worms. Sometimes, even a strong wind will send earthworms fleeing.

&ampersand; Humans take advantage of this behavior to collect earthworms. They rasp a wooden stick with a notched stick or coiled spring. This is called **grunting for worms.** Try it and see if the earthworms emerge!

&ampersand; Have you ever noticed what happens when you walk through a garden, backyard or park in the evening? If you look closely on the ground, you may notice earthworms crawling quickly into their holes in response to your footsteps.

&ampersand; Darwin, who studied earthworms most of his life, found that earthworms kept in clay pots on his piano would burrow when a certain chord was struck. This is another experiment you can try.

&ampersand; Earthworms have groups of cells all over their bodies which act as organs of touch. These cells have tiny projectile hairs that are sensitive to chemicals, temperature changes, and moisture conditions.

&ampersand; Earthworms have taste buds and show different food preferences. For example, they seem to prefer some manures over others. Design an experiment to find out what kind of food scraps they prefer.

Activity 2: Seeing is Believing

🐛 As students have already discovered, worms can sense light. They burrow down into the soil whenever the dark cloth is lifted from their bin. So how can they be observed doing their work? Worms don't seem to notice red light as much as other colors. The following demonstration will give students a chance to discover this fact, as well as introduce the spectrum of colors hidden in white light.

Purpose:

To see if worms notice some colors of light more than others.

Discovery Question:

How do worms react to different colors of light?

Materials:

worms
soil
white paper
prism
flashlight
rubber bands
food scraps in a glass container
different colors of acetate (large enough to be secured onto the
     flashlight with a rubber band) especially red, yellow, and
     blue

Procedure:

1) To demonstrate the hidden colors in white light, place a prism in a shaft of sunlight. Prisms bend the light, causing it to separate into its component parts, or wavelengths. White light is what we see when the sun shines - it is actually made up of all the different colors we know. A rainbow is a naturally occurring prism. When else have students seen the hidden colors in white light?

> *Creatures differ in their sensitivity to different colors, or wavelengths of light. Bees, for instance, can see ultraviolet light - they can see designs in flowers that resemble landing strips leading straight to the pollen. We can see these patterns only when a flower is viewed under UV light. Beavers, busily working in the dark, are not disturbed by red light, which we can see. Which wavelengths of light can worms see best? Which colors are invisible to them?*

2) With a small group of children, take white paper, flashlight, colored acetate, and the prism into the dark room where the worms are lying on top of the soil. Use the red filter first. Shine the red light on the worms. The worms should be happily moving on top of the soil, eating the food scraps.

3) Next, taking care not to shine the light onto the worms, change the color of the acetate. Try yellow next, (or whatever colors you may have), saving blue for last. Mix different combinations of acetate to see what colors you get. Observe the worms reactions to each of the colors.

> *Worms cannot "see" red light, so you should be able to observe them under red light. Most other colors will cause them to retreat into the soil. They are most sensitive to blue light, and will quickly hide in the soil when a blue light shines on them.*

Ask the children:
- How did the worms react to each color?
- What does this reaction say about their ability to see the color?
- What conclusions can students make about the worms sensitivity to different colors?

Results and Conclusions:

Children should record what they observe, and formulate their conclusions. Encourage them to illustrate their observations, for colorful drawings are more fun to look at and will trigger their memories in a different way than a written page.

Wormvision: How did earthworms react to light? Students can demonstrate their observations through illustrations, poetry, stories or dramatic presentations.

Extensions

Hidden Eyes: Children can find out which parts of an earthworm's body can detect light. They will need a flashlight, tape, a plate or tray, wet paper toweling, a dark room, and a piece of cardboard small enough to fit snugly into the head of the flashlight so that no light shines through.

1) Punch a pin-sized hole in the cardboard and tape it over the flashlight. Place the wet towel in the tray or plate. Put a worm on it, and leave it alone in the darkened room for a few minutes.

2) Shine the flashlight, which should be a very narrow beam of light, along the sides of the worm. Next try the back end, and finally the front.

3) What happens? An earthworm has clusters of light- sensitive cells in its front end. When the beam is directed toward this cluster, the worm will react by moving away.

(continued)

A Shadow in the Moon: Do worms react to a decrease in light? In the dark room, shine the flashlight on a worm for a few seconds until the worm stops wiggling. Then, slowly pass your hand over the flashlight. What happens? The worm should pull together suddenly. Why does the worm do this?

Discussion Questions

• Why don't you usually see earthworms during the day?

• What do earthworms do at night?

• If you wished to make careful observations of worms in the dark, what would you use to see them?

• How do the light-sensitive cells in the earthworm's front end help it find the surface of the ground?

• Earthworms will shrink in response to a decrease in light - caused, perhaps, by the shadow of a bird. Can you think of why this might be an important adaptation of earthworms?

• We can see better at night if we don't focus directly in front of us, but instead look out of the corners of our eyes. This is because special cells called **rods,** which help us see light and dark, are located on the edges of our retinas. (The **cones,** cells specialized for color, are concentrated in the center of the retina.) Students should try using the edge of their vision when walking at night.

• How do other animals "see" in the dark? How do you think ants, cats, owls, or bats travel about without running into things?

"Never Trust a Toad"

Elmira Earthworm was ecstatic, which means she was very - I mean **VERY** - excited. Marvin, the handsomest earthworm under the garden, had just asked her to marry him. Oh, she was in a fluster of excitement! She wiggled and wriggled and squiggled her way to the Wedding Dress Shop, beneath the maple tree.

Otto, the Toad, was the shop owner. Now, in case you didn't know, toads are rather fond of earthworms. They especially like earthworms for dessert, after a feast of flies. However, business was slow, so when Elmira came along Otto decided to forgo a meal for a chance to make some money.

Now for her part, Elmira was a rather silly girl, not too wise in the ways of the wild. The idea of a toad being dangerous never entered her head. Besides, she was on Cloud Nine, and all she could think of was her darling Marvin, and how lovely she would look in her wedding dress.

Elmira stepped into the shop and looked around. "I am looking for a wedding dress," she announced.

"That is the only kind we have here," replied Otto. "What size?"

"125 Segments long," she proudly answered.

(Segments were something Otto had never heard of, and he did not want to appear ignorant. Can you help him by telling him what a segment is?)

"Oh yes, I think I have something you might like." Otto thought about the 125 segments that made up Edmira's worm body. "Humm... that would make a tasty lunch, and I haven't had any breakfast," he thought to himself. "But first, lets see if I can make a sale!"

"Here you go!" he said cheerfully, choosing a white gown with lots of lace. He took the gown from a row of dresses designed to fit baby snakes.

"OOOh! It's lovely!" squealed Elmira, who rushed to try it on. Soon she came out in the long, flowing, lacy white dress. It fit her smoothly, except where her clitellum was. There, she had an odd bulge.

"Humm, perhaps you would like a girdle?" Otto suggested politely.

"Excuse me, this is my girdle, if you don't mind. I am rather proud of it! We earthworms also call it a band or clitellum. It's where our eggs form."

"Oh, then perhaps you would like a larger size?"

Elmira agreed. Unfortunately, as she tried to pull the dress over her head, the lace caught on her bristles. Otto tried to help her out of it by pulling with his webbed fingers.

What do you think happened? Well, the dress ripped to shreds. Otto the store owner looked at the ruined dress in dismay. He looked at Elmira with hungry eyes. Elmira must have sensed danger, for she crawled away as fast as she could - before Otto the Toad could snatch her for a meal!

Activity 3: The Great Gut Mystery

Purpose:

To solve some of the mysteries about an earthworm's internal anatomy.

Discovery Questions:

What are earthworms like on the inside? Do they have guts? Do they have a heart or lungs? How do they move if they have no bones?

Materials

worms for each pair of students
blank drawing paper
illustration of an earthworm's insides (Optional: see *Earthworms*, by K. Pigdon and M. Woolley.)
giant blank poster of earthworm interior anatomy located in appendix

Procedure

🐛 *You may wish to discuss with your children the ethics of dissecting worms. We strongly suggest that you do not perform a worm dissection as it contradicts a caring attitude toward worms. Worms are living beings, with nerves, five hearts, blood, and other internal organs. They feel pain and, being such delicate creatures, are easily harmed.*

1) Before looking at a picture of a worm's internal anatomy, have your children try to draw what they think is on the inside of the earthworm. There is no right or wrong in this exercise. Encourage them to draw what they imagine a worm's insides are like. What sorts of organs could possibly turn a banana peel into rich, fertile soil?

2) The teacher and students can take turns drawing the inside of the worm on the blackboard. Draw in and label the hearts, blood vessels, mouth, throat, gizzard, and food tube. Using colored chalk to show the different organs will help clarify the pictures. Students can copy the pictures into their journals.

3) The children can break up into 2 groups to research the following information. Each group should be responsible for either the **circulatory** or **digestive** systems. A short bibliography for this research is included at the end of this activity. Also, the school library may have additional resources on earthworms.

🙠 *The group as a whole needs to find a creative way to convey to the rest of the class the information they have researched. This can be done in a number of ways - through rap songs, music, puppet shows, or skits. These can be performed for the rest of the class, for parents, or for another class. Visual aids, such as student drawings and diagrams, are very helpful and can later be displayed in the classroom.*

Inside the Earthworm:

🙠 **Digestive System - a group of organs that break down food into nutrients (that help the animal grow and stay healthy) and waste products (that are eliminated).**

- What does a worm's digestive system do?
- What organs does it use in digestion?
- How does a worm's digestive system work?

🙠 **Digestion**

The earthworm's digestive tract is organized into different regions, each with a specialized function. The **pharynx** mixes and moistens the food. Muscular contractions push the food farther down the digestive tube into the **esophagus**. The esophagus secretes calcium carbonate, which neutralizes acids.

The food then moves on to the crop, where enzymes and bacteria break it into fine particles. These tiny food particles are further broken down in the **gizzard**. The gizzard has strong muscular walls that act like teeth. It uses sand to grind food particles into even smaller pieces. The gizzard also secretes a form of pepsin that digests proteins and starches. Finally, the food travels into the **intestine**, where intestinal juices complete the digestive process. Food is absorbed into the blood stream through the thin intestinal walls and then distributed to the cells.

❧ Circulatory System - A group of organs that pump blood to all parts of the body.

- What does the circulatory system do?
- What organs are used in a worm's circulatory system?
- How does the worms circulatory system work?

❧ Circulatory System

The earthworm has five contractile hearts. These are actually five pairs of enlarged blood vessels with valves that prevent the blood from backing up. The earthworm's blood contains a hemoglobin which transports oxygen. That is why earthworms have a pinkish tinge.

Earthworms breathe through their skin, which is why they need to be kept moist. Their bodies have mucus glands that secrete a substance that helps retain moisture.

Contrary to what many people think, earthworms can remain submerged in water for over an hour. The reason you see so many dead earthworms in puddles is probably due to sun exposure. One hour in the sun can paralyze a worm. Worms emerge from their burrows during a heavy rain because the water that has filtered down through the soil has very little oxygen. Also, carbon dioxide builds up when their burrows are sealed by water.

Activity Extensions

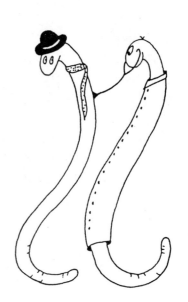

🐛 **My Guts:** Students can investigate their own digestive, circulatory and muscular systems and compare and contrast them with the worm's.

🐛 **Worm Anatomy Model:** Students might wish to make models of the worm's anatomy. They can use clay to make a three-dimensional model, paint a poster sized diagram, or make dioramas.

Resources for this project include:

Darling, Lois and Louis. *Worms*, William Morrow and Company, New York, NY, 1972.

McLaughlin, Mary. *Earthworms, Dirt and Rotten Leaves, An Exploration In Ecology*, Macmillan Publishing Company, New York, NY, 1986.

Pigdon, Keith and Marilyn, Woolley. *Earthworms*, Modern Curriculum Press, Cleveland, Ohio, 1989.

Simon, Seymour. *Discovering What Earthworms Do*, McGraw-Hill, New York, NY, 1969.

Activity 5: **The Great Gut Voyage**

Purpose:

    Children will review the internal anatomy of the earthworm by completing a story about an imaginary trip through an earthworm's body.

Materials:

    pencils and paper for writing
    paper and assorted art materials for drawing or painting

Procedure:

1) Read the following story to the students.

2) Challenge students to complete the story on their own or in groups of two. They may also illustrate their stories.

3) Instead of having each student write the entire story on her own, you might want to break the voyage into mini-adventures. For example, from the mouth to the crop, from the crop to the gizzard, gizzard to intestine, intestine to blood vessels, blood vessels to hearts, hearts to intestine, and down the intestine and out. You can break it up in any way that makes sense to you and your students. This alternative makes for a more detailed writing experience. It could also be the basis for an educational skit.

> **Note:** You might want to have a picture on the blackboard that traces the path of the voyage.

"The Great Gut Voyage"

Imagine you have just eaten your favorite forbidden food, something your parents never let you have except on special occasions. But this is not a special occasion. You are sneaking it, sitting in your tree house on a sunny summer afternoon. Oh, it tastes so delicious! As the last bits of this treat linger in your mouth, you sigh with contentment and close your eyes for awhile. Suddenly you look up and notice that the tree house seems to be getting larger. And the tree is humongous! Look at the size of those birch leaves! What is happening? The ground looks awfully far away. How will you ever get down?

The nails holding the tree house together are as big as you are, and leaves are the size of a house! Things are getting bigger still - or are you shrinking? To your left you see a spider larger than anything you have ever seen! Its hairy legs, bulbous, beady eyes and gigantic menacing jaws are like something out of a horror movie. But this is no movie - this is your real life! Without hesitating, you drag a birch leaf to the edge of the tree house, push it over the edge, and, just as it is about to go sailing free in the air, you jump on for a ride.

Slowly, you drift down to the soft grass below. You have plenty of time to notice that the veins in the leaf are thicker than your arm. You land with a soft swish. You find yourself in a forest - no, a jungle - of grass taller than the tallest skyscraper you have ever seen, monstrous insects, boulders, mountains of dirt, canyons, caves, and deep, endless pits that look as wide as a football field.

As you look into a deep hole, trying not to fall in, something . . . something seemingly huge and horrible begins to emerge from it. What on earth? It's only an earthworm, but you have shrunk to the size of a grain of sand so the creature seems deadly. To think - just this morning you were feeding the friendly worms in your classroom!

Luckily, the earthworm happens to be Omar, Wilma's favorite brother. He writes to Wilma weekly at the Earthworm Compost Farm in your classroom! He senses you are there, even though he cannot see images the way humans can. "Who is there?" he asks in a friendly voice.

You explain to him your situation, and immediately he has a great idea. He can mail you in his letter - right to your classroom! You crawl into the envelope, and are whisked off to the Earthworm Post Office. Omar writes a special message to Wilma, and on the envelope writes "Handle With Care".

After a long sleep, you wake to find yourself covered with blankets beside a blazing fire in Wilma Worm's living room. Wilma sees that you are no longer sleeping and greets you with some leaf mash. Normally this wouldn't be very appealing, but you have not eaten for two days, and you are starving.

Wilma introduces herself. She tells you that she has been talking your situation over with your family, teacher and classmates. If you agree, you can go on an amazing adventure never before experienced by a human being. If you eat a little more of that forbidden food (you left an extra piece in your jacket), you will shrink even further. You can then get into a capsule designed by scientists, and travel down an earthworm's gullet!

All is set several days later. You will shrink to an almost invisible size, then climb into a capsule that looks like a miniature submarine. Leadbelly, the biggest earthworm in the bin, will swallow the submarine capsule and your adventure will begin! You will travel through his throat and down a long thin tube into his crop, where food is sometimes stored for awhile. Then you will slide into his gizzard, where the food is chopped up (the submarine is designed to withstand the forces of the gizzard), and on into his intestine.

Teeny, weeny blood vessels which absorb the nutrients that help earthworms grow, wrap around the intestine. The wall between the intestine and the blood vessels is so thin it is possible to move through them in your submarine - just as the nutrients do. From this point you will be carried in the blood to one of the five hearts. Earthworms do not have four-chambered hearts the way we do. Their hearts are actually enlarged blood vessels that work together to squeeze the earthworm's blood through the length of its body.

Blood has four jobs. One is to carry nutrients it picked up in the intestine to all the cells in the earthworms body. Another is to carry the oxygen the earthworm absorbs through its skin to all the cells. So every cell in the worm's body is constantly being given nutrients and oxygen. The other two jobs are to carry wastes and carbon dioxide from the cells out of the worm's body. Blood works in our own body to do the same things - to carry nutrients and oxygen to each cell, and to carry wastes and carbon dioxide away.

After you visit the hearts, you will be carried back to the intestines. You will then continue in your midget submarine down the intestinal tube until you are eliminated with Leadbelly's casting. What an exciting adventure this is going to be!

Hop into your submarine and get ready, get set! Gulp!

🙠 *What happens? Write a story about your adventure through the earthworm's insides!*

Chapter 5:

A Year In The Life Of The Worm

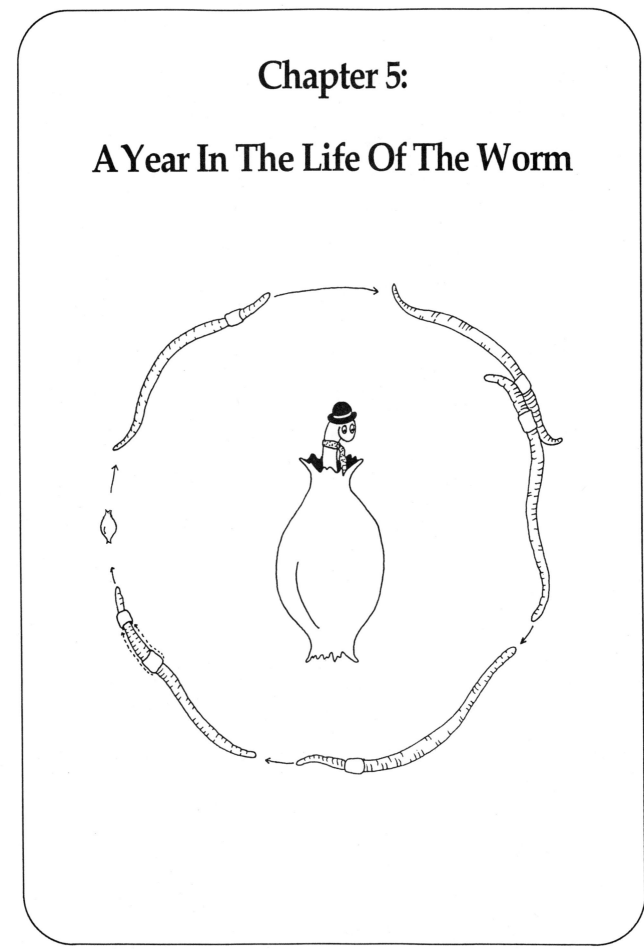

Chapter 5:

A Year In The Life Of The Worm

🐛 This section introduces students to the earthworm's life cycle and population balances.

Table of Contents   **Page**

Activity 1: Banded Breeders, or Worms Wear Girdles!

Purpose:

Children familiarize themselves with the earthworms' life cycle through observation and inquiry.

Materials

> 1 pie plate for each group of 2-3 children
> water
> several worms kept covered on wet pie plates until observed
> if possible, several examples of cocoons (worm "eggs")
> mating worms, if possible
> hand lenses
> paper and pencils for sketching

Procedure

1) During this activity, ask students to record and sketch each characteristic they notice and to observe any similarities or differences.

2) Place several worms on a wet pie plate and ask the children to observe and record details.

🐛 Aside from size, students may discover that some of the worms have a swollen region 1/3 of the distance between the head and the tail. Make sure that each student gets a chance to observe this area, known as the *girdle* or *band*. Scientists call it a *clitellum*. The band is characteristic of a sexually mature worm.

3) Discuss with students:

> • What is this swollen area?
> • Can you determine which worms are male and which are female?

🐛 *There are no "male" and "female" worms.*

All worms have both sperm and eggs, but they must exchange sperm in order to mate. Sometimes it is possible to observe mating worms; it might be worth while to find some mating worms before beginning this lesson. If not, refer to the Chapter 5 cover, "A Year in the Life of the Worm" at the beginning of this activity. Encourage the childen to draw and label the worms.

5) Earthworm cocoons can be easily observed with a hand lens. If children look carefully, they may see the baby worms inside and, sometimes, bright red blood vessels pumping away!

 *The **cocoon,** a type of egg case, is home for as many as four developing worms. Soon after mating, a cocoon, filled with fertilized eggs, slips off the clitellum. It slides down to the end of the worm's body, then drops off. As it does, both ends of the cocoon close off, and it becomes a protective, hardened case. It is about the size of a grain of rice, resembles a small apple seed, and may be found among the soil particles. As the baby worm develops over a three week period, the cocoon changes from pearly white to yellow to brown. Students are very good at finding earthworm cocoons!*

6) Ask the children to identify a cocoon, a baby and a mature worm. Sometimes it is possible to watch baby worms emerge from their cocoon. Students can search on their pie plates for the youngest worm. Newly-hatched worms are whitish-pink and almost transparent. Typically, they are 1/2 inch to an inch long. How long is the smallest worm? Which group thinks it has the youngest worm? Who has the biggest (and maybe the oldest) worm? Ask the children to place their worms in order from the youngest to the oldest.

7) Students can make final sketches of what they have observed. These illustrations can be saved in their earthworm journals. In addition, they might want to make a poster showing the different stages of a worm's life cycle.

Extensions

🐛 **Life Cycle Skit** - Act out different stages of the life cycle, from co-coon formation to birth to adult worm. This could include movement, music, and art.

🐛 **Worm Talk** - Write up a mock interview of an earthworm's life. This can be based on a combination of fact and fiction. How long does an earthworm live? What does it do in the winter? How many children, grandchildren, great-grandchildren, nieces, nephews, etc. does it have? What special features does its burrow have? What do earthworms do at parties?

🐛 **My Life As A Worm** - Write a short story about the life of an elder worm. Memories . . . .

Activity 2:

Worm Math: Will Earthworms Take Over The World?

Purpose:

Students will discover the amazing reproductive capacity of earthworms, and then (in activity 3) will discuss natural population balances.

Materials:

pencils and paper

Procedure

1) If a worm lays 2 cocoons a week, and 2 hatchlings emerge from each cocoon, how many new worms will you have in 3 weeks? ($2 \times 2 \times 3 = 12$)

2) If a worm lays 3 cocoons a week, and 1 hatchling emerges from each cocoon, how many worms will you have in 4 weeks?
($3 \times 1 \times 4 = 12$)

3) If a worm lays 3 cocoons a week, and 3 hatchlings emerge from each, how many earthworms will you have in 2 weeks?
($3 \times 3 \times 2 = 18$)

4) If a worm lays 2 cocoons a week, and 2 hatchlings emerge from each, how many worms will you have in 4 weeks?
 ($2 \times 2 \times 4 = 16$)

5) If a worm lays 2 cocoons a week, and 2 hatchlings emerge from each, how many worms will you have in 10 weeks?
($2 \times 2 \times 10 = 40$)

6) If 10 worms each produce 40 hatchlings, how many baby worms do they make all together? ($10 \times 40 = 400$)

7) If a single worm can make 200 baby worms a year, how many baby

worms will 10 worms make in a year? (10 x 200 = 2000)
- How many baby worms will 100 worms make?
(100 x 200 = 20,000)
- What about 1000 worms? (1000 x 200 = 200,000)

8) If 1000 worms make 200,000 babies a year, it is only the tip of the iceberg! Don't forget, all these babies will produce babies too! (So why don't worms take over the world???)

Remember this from your Amazing Facts List?

&❧ **Earthworm population growth rate** - 10 worms will double in one month, increase to 640 worms in six months, become 10,240 worms in ten months, and will expand to 40,960 worms in a year! How many worms would you have in a year if you started with 1000 worms? If you started with 10 worms, how many earthworms would you have after 3 years?

Activity 3: A Healthy, Happy Home

Purpose:

In this activity, children will be given the opportunity to discuss some of the natural factors involved in worm population balance.

Materials:

Newsprint and chart for listing ideas

Procedure:

Discuss the following questions with your group:

1) What do you think a worm needs to move, eat, and grow? What might happen if its space got too crowded? How do you feel in a crowded place?

2) Brainstorm a list of what worms need in order to survive. Make sure to include the following: food, water, shelter/cover, space, and a clean environment.

3) Discuss each of these needs and come up with lists about why each need is important. Include in this discussion:

- How much water does a worm need?
- What is the worm's shelter or home in the classroom? In the natural world?
- Does a worm need a healthy, clean environment in which to live? Why?
- What are some examples of worm food?
- How do worms' needs change from season to season?
- How do the needs of worms compare to the needs of other species, such as ants, frogs, or people?

4) What kinds of things might pollute a worm's environment in the natural world? What might contaminate it in the Earthworm Compost Farm?

*Did you know a worm enriches the soil with its **castings**, or droppings? Unfortunately for the worm, these castings are toxic to it. That is why every six months it is a good idea to change the soil in your Earthworm Compost Farm. In nature, worms will actually migrate to a new area when their homes become overcrowded or polluted.*

5) Could your worm farm explode and spill over with worms? Would there always be enough food, water, space, and clean soil for them to live happily?

Background information - Basic Needs

🐛 The availability of food, water, space, proper temperature, and clean soil influence how many worms can live in a certain area. These basic needs act to control population growth. If one of these is out of balance - such as food - the population will be limited or may decline. If there is not enough or too much water, all the worms could die. Our earthworm friends are not found everywhere, and in fact are quite choosy about their living spaces. Have you ever wondered why you don't find worms at the beach, in the desert, and why you might find worms in your back yard but not in your friend's yard? These elements that control population growth are called **limiting factors**.

ꙮ Worms do not like their homes to be polluted. Although they enrich the soil with their castings, their castings are also poisonous to them. Other sources of pollution, such as pesticides, herbicides, and artificial fertilizers probably do a lot to keep the worm population down. In fact, these poisons sometimes eliminate worm populations altogether.

Activity Extensions:

ꙮ **Worm Mania:**
Could worms really take over the world? What do students think? Challenge them to write a short story!

ꙮ **Worms to the Rescue:**
What can be done to preserve or create abundant earthworm populations and healthy soil?

Students can design habitat improvement projects in poor soils. When the weather warms up, dig up soils in your school or community (with permission, of course!).

How healthy, or fertile, are the soils? Students can assess different samples. Is the soil rich, dark, and full of earthworms? Are there plants growing in it? Or is it sandy or clay-like, and devoid of plants? These things indicate infertile soil.

After determining the fertility of the soil, students can suggest ways of creating a richer soil. If possible, encourage students to implement their idea. Have them keep track of their plots over time and see what happens!

Chapter 6:

Exploring The Earthworm Farm Community

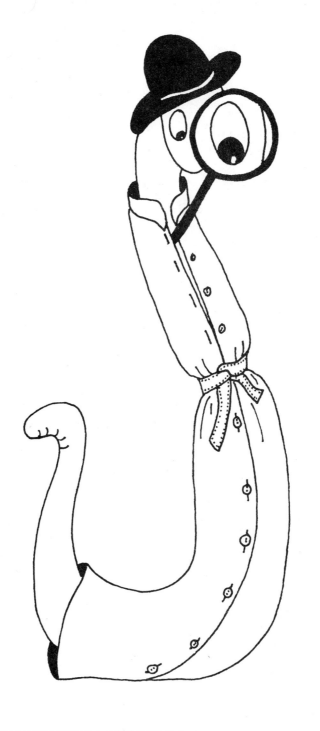

Chapter 6

Exploring The Earthworm Compost Farm Community

What else besides earthworms lurks within the dark depths of the Earthworm Compost Farm? Do earthworms work alone to break down organic matter, or do other living things feed off the decaying vegetation in the Earthworm Compost Farm? Could the Earthworm Compost Farm be home for any earthworm predators? In this chapter, students will carefully explore the vermicompost for signs of large and small creatures that may share the earthworms' home.

Table of Contents   **Page**

Activity 1

Other Beasties In The Bin

Purpose:

In this activity, children explore other creatures that might turn up in the Earthworm Compost Farm.

> **Note:** Some Earthworm Compost Farms do not contain an abundance of other creatures. Either the soil is sterile, or the bin is stored in a location that does not attract other critters. If you wish to study the Earthworm Compost Farm food web in detail, you might expose a mini-bin to the damp elements of an old cellar (especially one with a dirt floor). Make sure the temperature does not fall below 55 degrees F. and remember to feed and water the worms!

Discovery Question:

Do earthworms share their home with any other creatures?

Materials:
pie plates
hand lenses
good light source
paper and pencil for drawing

Procedure:

1) Take handfuls of soil from different areas within the bin (near the top, in the center, toward the sides) and place them on plates. Have the students pick out the earthworms and put them back into the bin. Label each plate, noting the area of the bin the sample came from.

2) Using hand lenses under a good light source, have pairs of children gently probe the soil with their fingers, looking for little bugs in the soil. When they find a creature, have them isolate it and observe it carefully. One child can verbally describe it, while the other child writes down the description.

3) If they are interested, have students identify the creatures they find.

> **Note:** Most of the creatures the children will find are vegetarians which feed on the decaying plant matter. Centipedes, the only predators that might be found in the bin, kill worms. Centipedes may pinch, so handle with care!

Activity 2: Magnificent Micro-critters!

Purpose:

Children can explore the microscopic life that lives in the Earthworm Compost Farm. Bacteria, protozoa, nematodes and rotifers are important parts of the food web that help to break down the food the larger creatures eat.

Discovery Questions:

Are there creatures living in the earthworm bin that are so small they can't be seen with the naked eye? What do these creatures look like?

Materials:

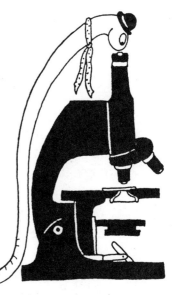

Procedure A
petri dishes
water
petri dish and cover
soil from Earthworm Compost Farm
bread crumbs
a warm place to incubate petri dish sample

Procedure B
wide mouth jar
soil from Earthworm Compost Farm
cheesecloth
eyedropper
microscope slide
microscope
egg yolk

Procedure:

A) Either the teacher or the students can try to isolate the **microorganisms** (tiny creatures that cannot be seen with the naked eye). First, take a petri dish and mix soil from the Earthworm Compost Farm with bread crumbs. Moisten with a little water, put on the cover, and store in a warm place for a week. When the week is over, students can look at the petri dish under the microscope and draw what they see.

B) Another method of isolating microorganisms is to create "soil water". Fill a jar with clean tap water. Wrap a soil sample in cheese cloth and place it in the jar of water. Allow it to sit for 24 hours. Using an eyedropper, place a drop of soil water on a slide and view it under the microscope.

🐛 If few microorganisms are present, place a tablespoon or two of soil into a baby food jar, add a bit of hard boiled egg yolk, shake, and cover. Place in a dark spot at room temperature for a few days. The egg yolk enriches the soil water. This allows microorganisms to multiply and become easier to see.

> **Note:** Trying to draw microorganisms suspended in water can be difficult or frustrating for the students. Students can just look at the slides and draw from memory.

🐛 Encourage students to draw what they see, or let them simply observe the phenomena. This is a chance for them to explore the different kinds of creatures hidden in the soil. Identification is not necessary.

Activity Extensions:

🐛 **Earthworm Compost Farm Food Web:** Students may wish to create a food web or a food chain for the Earthworm Compost Farm. Display a model of these in the classroom.

🐛 **Miming Microcritters:** Students might like to mime different critters and have other students guess what they are trying to mime.

Magnificent Micro-Critters!

1. Observe the soil in the petri dish under a microscope. What do you see? Draw it here.

2. View the slide of the soil under the microscope. What do you see? Draw it here.

Chapter 7

What's Better Than A Genie In A Bottle?

Chapter 7

What's Better Than A Genie In A Bottle?

🐦 In this chapter, children make earthworm apartment houses (miniature Earthworm Compost Farms), from recycled plastic soda bottles. As a follow-up exploration, students create a mini-ecosystem with a plant, some soil and the earthworm.

The directions for the bottle cuts are courtesy of:

Bottle Biology
Center for Biology Education
B-37 Russell Laboratories
1630 Linden Drive, Madison WI. 53706.

Table Of Contents   Page

Activity 1: Earthworm Apartment Houses

Purpose:

In this project, children construct an earthworm apartment house from recycled plastic soda bottles to sit on their desks. In addition, children observe and experiment with the composting process.

Materials for each column:

three 2 liter plastic soda bottles with caps for each
      column
hot tap water
knife
scissors
magic marker
paper clips, or awls
gloves for handling hot paper clips
candle and matches
paper fasteners
mosquito netting or lightweight, black screen
rubber bands
soil and vermiculite
compostable and non-compostable materials, such as
      kitchen scraps, grass clippings, leaves, news-
      papers, plastic, or metal utility knife for each
      adult

> **Note:** A ratio of 5 children to 1 adult is recommended, as the procedure may be confusing. A number of steps in this procedure require supervision. Only adults should handle utility knives.

❧ Each child may work alone to create her own compost column or earthworm apartment house that will sit on her desk. Alternatively, children may break into groups of two to construct and share the column.

Procedure

1) Children should remove labels and bases from the bottles. To do this, have them fill bottles about 3/4 full with very hot water, recap and allow to sit for a few minutes. This allows the glue that holds the base of the bottle and the label to soften, making them easier to remove.

2) Turn two of the bottles upside down and twist off the black plastic base. Leave the base on the third bottle. Remove labels from all three bottles.

3) Students pour out the water and mark bottles as follows:

Bottle #1: Draw a line around the bottle near the top where the sides taper and another line at the bottom where the sides begin to taper.

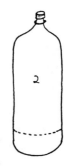

Bottle #2: Draw a line at the bottom where the sides taper.

Bottle #3: This is the bottle with the intact base. Draw a line about 1/2 way up the sides.

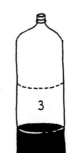

4) Using a utility knife, start the cuts for the students. Have them carefully finish with scissors along the lines they drew.

5) Have the students place the wire mesh screening over the top of the second bottle and secure as shown in the illustration. This will allow for drainage.

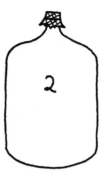

6) The students can now assemble the column as shown in the illustration. Secure the bottles together with masking or duct tape. Tape the left-over top to bottle #1. This will serve as the "door" to the apartment house.

7) Remind students that *air* is important for both the earthworms and the soil. To get air into the earthworm column, students will need to make holes through the plastic at various points in the top of two of the bottles. Students can do this by using the awl, or adults can punch the holes with the utility knife. Poke 6 or 7 holes around both 1 and 2. *Please supervise students as they do this!*

8) Add bedding material, such as a mixture of peat moss, vermiculite, mature compost, and leaf mold through the top of bottle #1. Continue adding material until bottle #1 is filled halfway. A handful of vermiculite mixed in with the bedding will help aerate the soil.

Note: Vermiculite is important to help aerate the soil.

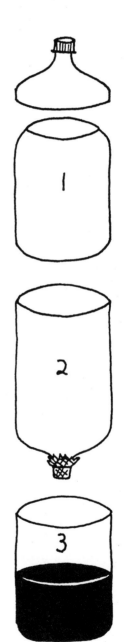

9) Gently place a handful of worms into their new home and feed them kitchen scraps. Remind students that the soil must be kept moist (but not wet) or else the worms will die. Remember:

- earthworms need the moisture to breathe.
- earthworms like darkness, so each column should be covered with dark paper to keep out the light.
- earthworms are always hungry and need to be fed regularly.

10) Students can place the earthworm columns on their desks and make daily observations of "their" co-owned earthworm apartment house.

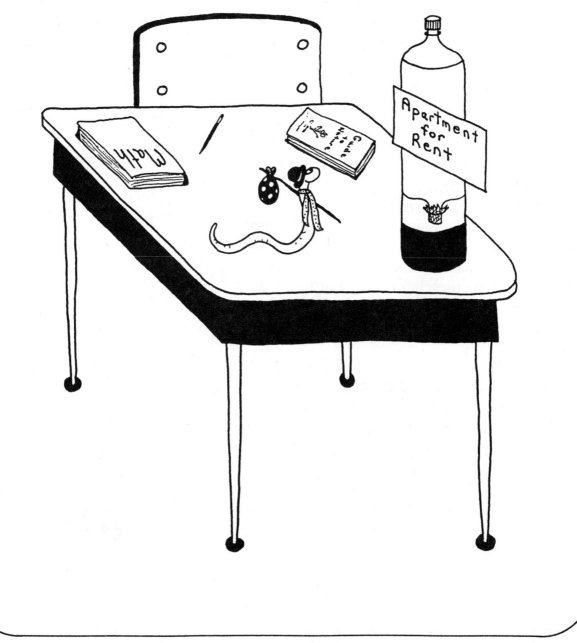

Activity 2: A Trio of Friends -
The Earthworm, The Soil, And The Plant

Purpose:

The students explore the interrelationship between the plant, earthworm and soil.

Materials:

earthworm apartment house
vermicompost (soil from Earthworm Compost Farm)
seed or seedling

Procedure:

1) Students can choose a plant to grow inside the worm's apartment house. Appropriate plants include: spider plant-cutting, mini-marigolds, or any seedling they would like. Or plant a seed - such as orange, grapefruit, radish, or a bean seed - and see what happens.

2) Next, have students gently drop the plant or seed through the top of the column and carefully tamp it down into the soil. The eraser end of a pencil is a great tool for doing this!

3) Students should feed the earthworms chopped up leaves, dropped on top of the soil. They can watch the plant grow along with the earthworms. Mention to students that if this were a larger plant, it would be dropping leaves to feed the earthworm.

4) After a month students should dismantle the apartment houses and gently return the earthworms to their home on the Earthworm Compost Farm. If they are careful as they take apart the apartment house, they can save the seedling and transplant it into a pot.

5) Invite the students to draw a web of life showing the relationship between worms, soil, moisture, and plants. Have them consider: Why should we put a plant in the earthworm apartment house?

    🐛 *The earthworms help enrich the soil for the plant, the plant helps keep the soil moist, and the plant roots hold the soil together.*

6) Students might like to illustrate the relationship between the soil, a plant, and earthworms. These drawings can be placed in their journals for safe keeping.

Chapter 8:

Earthworm Extensions: What, No Earthworms??

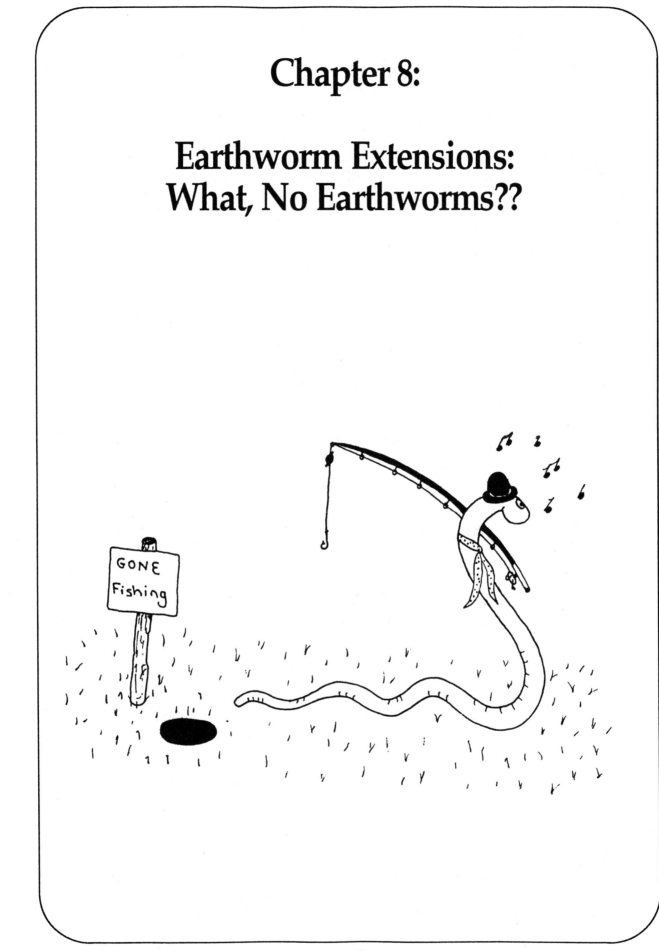

Chapter 8:

Earthworm Extensions: What, No Earthworms??

 Earthworms are the world's best composters, but compost can be made by humans too! This chapter contains activities that explore indoor composting without the help of earthworms. The *Student Experimental Method Discovery Sheet* may be used for any of the experiments in this chapter.

Explorations and Experiments

My Discovery question: What will happen if . . . ?

My Prediction: What I think will happen is . . . .

My Data: **(Observations/Measurements)** What happened was . . . .

My Conclusion: I learned that . . . .

Activity 1: Constructing Compost Columns

Purpose:

Children observe and experiment with the composting process without the help of earthworms by constructing a compost column from recycled plastic soda bottles.

> **Note:** A ratio of 5 children to 1 adult is recommended for this activity. A number of steps in this procedure require supervision - only adults should handle utility knives.

🐛 Each child may make his own compost column that will sit on his desk. Or children may break into groups of two to construct and share a column.

Materials for each child:

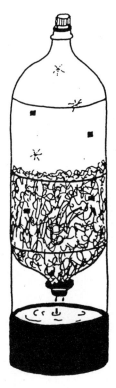

three 2-liter plastic soda bottles for each
     column, with caps
hot tap water
knife
scissors
magic marker
paper clips, or awls
gloves for handling hot paper clips
candle and matches
paper fasteners
mosquito netting or lightweight black
     screen
rubber bands
soil
compostable and non-compostable
     materials, such as kitchen scraps,
     grass clippings, leaves, newspapers,
     plastic, or metal
utility knife for each adult

Procedure:

1) Students should remove labels and bases from the bottles. To do this, have them fill bottles about 3/4 full with very hot water, recap, and allow to sit for a few minutes. This softens glue that holds the base of the bottle and the label, making it easier to remove them.

2) Turn two of the bottles upside down and twist off the black plastic bases. Leave the base on the third bottle. Remove labels on all three bottles.

3) Students pour out the water and mark bottles as follows:

Bottle #1: Draw a line around the bottle near the top, where the sides taper, and another line at the bottom where the sides begin to taper.

Bottle #2: Draw a line at the bottom where the sides taper.

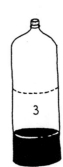

Bottle #3: This is the bottle with the intact base. Draw a line about 1/2 way up the sides.

4) Using a utility knife, start cuts for students. Have students use scissors to finish cutting along the lines they drew.

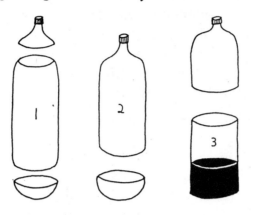

5) Have the students place the wire mesh screening over the top of the second bottle and secure as shown in the illustration. This will allow for drainage.

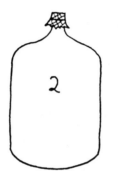

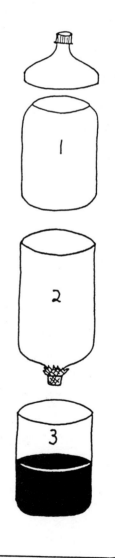

6) Next, have the students assemble the column as shown in the illustration.

7) Add soil and compostable materials, such as grass clippings, lunch box items, kitchen scraps, or leaves. Layer in equal amounts. In addition, put in some non-compostable materials, such as plastic, metal, rubber, or aluminum foil. Students should record in their journals exactly what they put in the columns.

Note: Students must open the lid of the column every two or three days to check moisture. They should stir the compost contents thoroughly, with a spoon, adding water if necessary.

🐛 These compost bottles may be kept on desks for daily observation. Children can describe with as much detail as possible what they see. They should especially be on the lookout for any changes in temperature, contents, condensation, and so on. Temperature checks may be taken with soil thermometers.

🐛 In addition, children might wish to make hypotheses, or guesses, about what they think will happen in the compost process. They can use the following questions as guidelines to formulate a hypothesis.

- Will some materials take longer to compost than others?
- Which things will compost fastest?
- Which ones will compost more slowly?

🐛 As a review, ask the children to draw a diagram explaining the compost process.

🐛 Once a week, children can pour out some of the contents that have been composting. They should describe the contents, paying close attention to smells, kinds of materials they see, any seeds that may be germinating, color of soil, size and shape of the particles, and materials not yet composted.

Background Information

🐛 As living things grow, they absorb nutrients. Plants take up nutrients directly from the soil, and animals get their nutrients by eating plants or other animals. When a plant or animal dies, it decomposes and returns nutrients to the soil. Soil microorganisms, such as fungi and bacteria, work to decompose dead plants and animals. This breakdown of plants and animals allows nutrients to be recycled, or to be returned to the soil whence they originally came.

🐛 The Earthworm Compost Farm and composting are two forms of nutrient cycling. In both situations, special conditions are created that accelerate the process of breaking down organic matter into its component parts.

Activity 2: The Great Compost Race

Purpose:

To see if all organic materials decompose at the same rates.

Discovery Question:

Do all organic materials decompose at the same rate?

Materials:

compost columns
grass clippings
leaves
soil
water
orange rinds
apple cores
banana peels
bread
paper
tea bag
cardboard
newspaper
natural sponges

The Great Compost Race

On Your Marks...
Get Set...

Procedure:

1) Challenge the children to predict which items will break down into their component parts first.

2) Make 3 or 4 compost columns, following steps 1-9 of Activity 1.

3) Set up the experiment as before, with one control and 3 or 4 test columns. Students should place a variety of organic materials into the control column.

4) In each of the test columns, have students place a different organic item and predict how long it will take for that item to break down into its component parts.

> **Note:** Make sure all other variables such as light, temperature, moisture, and frequency of mixing are consistent.

5) How did student predictions compare with the results?

> _Important_: Remind the children that the accuracy of their guesses is not as significant as the process of guessing, testing, and discovering what happens. If the results of the experiment were different than they expected, then they learned something new!

6) Encourage the children to create another experiment testing the compost time of different materials.

The winners are the Losers!

Activity Extensions:

    ❧ Create a **skit** around the results of The Great Compost Race. You might think of using a race as a metaphor. Students can place bets on their favorite compostable item.

    Alternatively, they may make up costumes representing different compostable items. One by one they can disappear into the "compost pile" (perhaps a black cloth). The items that compost most rapidly can pop out first, followed by those that break down more slowly.

    ❧ Make an **educational poster** about the fastest compost items in the East.

Activity 3: Stirring Up The Pot

Purpose:

Children determine how often compost needs to be mixed.

Discovery Questions:

Will mixing compost at different frequencies affect the compost process? How?

Materials:

compost columns
soil
kitchen scraps
spoons for stirring

Procedure:

1) Ask the children to predict the following: Will mixing compost at different frequencies effect the compost process? How?

2) Label 6 compost columns, A-F. Fill them with layers of soil and kitchen scraps.

3) Mix the contents of the columns with the following frequency:

column A - twice a day
column B - once a day
column C - twice a week
column D - once a week
column E - once every two weeks
column F - no mixing at all

4) After about three weeks, pour out the contents from the different bottles and examine the compost. It might help to put the different columns on separate tables covered with newspaper. Make signs that tell how often the compost was stirred.

5) The children can break up into small groups and move from table to table to examine the compost, record observations, put together data and come up with conclusions. They may use the observation sheet on the next page.

Extensions

🐾 **Variables:** What would happen if we didn't water the compost, or if we watered it too much? Is there an ultimate amount of **water** that should be used? What would be the effect of various **temperatures** on the process? Have the students create experiments to test these questions.

🐾 Conduct a **Master Column Composter Mini-Conference.** Interview various "master column composters" about their views on the best mixing, temperature, and moisture conditions for compost columns. Or students can give workshops on their favorite techniques for indoor composting in columns.

Stirring Up The Pot

Mixed	Observations
Two times a day	
Once a day	
Two times a week	
Once a week	
Every two weeks	
Not mixed	

Activity 4: To Compost Or Not To Compost?

Purpose:

Children conduct an experiment to explore the difference between organic and inorganic materials.

Discovery Question:

What is the difference between organic and inorganic materials?

Materials:

compost columns (3 or 4 columns for each group of children)
grass clippings
leaves
soil
water
plants
metal
rubber bands
cardboard
aluminum foil
newspaper
sponges
other materials

Prediction:

Children guess which materials will compost and which ones will not.

Note: Depending on available materials, the experiment can be organized in one of two ways. If two children wish to work together, they can make as many columns as they need to carry out their experiments. Alternatively, 3 or 4 children may wish to collaborate, sharing their personal columns as part of a group experiment. Directions to construct compost columns are in Activity 1 of this chapter.

Procedure:

1) Ask the children if they know what determines whether or not a material can or cannot be composted. Using the above list, challenge them to predict which items will compost and which ones will not.

2) This experiment will need a **control column** (one composting column similar to the previous experiment), and 2 to 3 other **test columns** (a) to compare the compost rate of different materials, and (b) to test whether or not the material can actually be composted.

3) Set up the columns so they have equal amounts of starting material - grass clippings, leaves, soil, and water. They should also be exposed to the same environmental variables - light, temperature, and moisture. The only difference between columns will be the test materials Materials can be added to all but the control column. Test materials include plastic, metal, rubber bands, cardboard, newspaper, aluminum foil, or sponges.

4) Ask the students to make a hypothesis about which materials will break down and which ones won't. Once a week, remove and examine the contents of each bottle.

5) At the conclusion of the experiment, see if they can explain why some materials break down and some do not.

> **Background Information:** The reason some things break down into their original components and others do not is due to the nature of the materials. If an object is **organic,** that means it is derived from living matter. Organic matter contains carbon and can be decomposed into basic elements. **Inorganic** objects, because they are not made from living matter, cannot be broken down as easily. They are composed of matter that is mineral in origin, and usually do not contain carbon.

&If the children have a difficult time understanding the difference between organic and inorganic materials, explain the concepts to them using specific examples from each. Then place several items, both organic and inorganic, in one pile and ask the students to separate them into their respective groups.

Activity 5: Composting Used News

Purpose:

To explore an alternative way to deal with used newspapers.

Materials:
> compost columns
> shredded newspaper
> soil
> water

Procedure:
1) Have students create an experiment using two columns. Fill one with a mixture of shredded newspaper and soil. The other should be filled with the same amount of shredded newspaper, but no soil. Remind them to plan occasional rainstorms over the columns so that they will remain moist.

2) Students should mix the contents twice weekly so air gets into the process.

3) After 3 or 4 weeks, students can pour out the contents and answer the following questions.

Concluding Discussion Questions:

🐛 Which method worked best to compost the newspaper (the column with soil or the column without soil)? Why do you think this method worked best?

🐛 How can we apply this information to the problem of what to do with used newspapers? (Farmers are beginning to use shredded newspaper for animal bedding).

🐛 What do you do with used newspapers? Brainstorm all the things you could do with used newspapers. Produce a skit demonstrating what to do with used news.

Chapter 9:

Culminating Activities

Celebrating the Wonderful World of Wigglers

Chapter 9:

Culminating Activities

🐌 Culminating Activities bring together in a satisfying, tangible way, the skills that the children have been working on. Culminating projects offer an alternative to testing by demonstrating newly gained skills and information through practical applications.

Table Of Contents   Page

Activity 1: Vive la Difference!

Purpose:

This activity explores and compares the different processes by which compost piles and the Earthworm Compost Farm break down food waste. It gives children the opportunity to put together the concepts they have been learning through the activities in the "Wonderful World of Wigglers."

Background:

There are two significant differences between a compost pile and an Earthworm Compost Farm. Firstly, the organisms breaking down the food are different. Composting in the pile occurs with the help of **microorganisms** - fungi and bacteria. The Earthworm Compost Farm is inhabited primarily by earthworms, which are considered **macroorganisms**. Bacteria and fungi are present, but in smaller numbers than in the compost pile.

The different organisms result in very different temperature patterns during the composting process. The fungi and bacteria present in a compost pile eat away at the food scraps and produce heat. This heating does not occur in the Earthworm Compost Farm - in fact, it would probably kill the earthworms.

Since temperature is an important factor in the compost process, the compost pile works only during the warmer months. The Earthworm Compost Farm is usually an indoor project, so decomposition can occur any time of year.

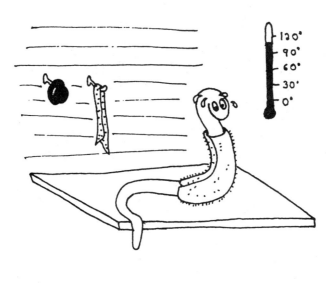

Materials:

Earthworm Compost Farm
compost column

Procedure:

1) If possible, juxtapose the Earthworm Compost Farm and a compost column in view of the children. Begin by having the children think of everything they know about, or associate with, the Earthworm Compost Farm. Ask them questions to help bring out ideas.

a) What temperatures do earthworms like? 55-70 degrees F.

b) What organisms are most active in the earthworm bin community? Millipedes, centipedes, sow bugs, mites, springtails, ants, fruit flies, and - last but not least - earthworms. Bacteria and fungi are present, as in compost, but in fewer numbers.

c) What ingredients do you need to start the Earthworm Compost Farm? Bedding, (such as shredded newspaper or computer strips, shredded corrugated cardboard, animal manures, peat moss, leaf mold), water, and worms.

d) What happens to the food scraps you put into the earthworm bin? It is consumed and transformed into nutrient-rich soil by earthworms. The earthworms have some help from other creatures in the bin (as well as fungi and bacteria). They eat the food and transform it into rich soil.

e) What can you do with the soil that is created by the earthworms? Use it to fertilize house plants, or use it to start your seeds. Make gifts of potted plants in vermicompost! Sell it as is, or give it away as gifts to elders for their house plants.

f) What time of year is best for an indoor Earthworm Compost Farm? Any time of year, but it works out well if you do it when you are not composting outdoors. Set up the Earthworm Compost Farm as you are doing your last outdoor compost run, and then feed your food scraps to the earthworms! As spring turns into summer and the temperatures become suitable for composting, you can turn the contents of the Earthworm Compost Farm - earthworms and all - onto your garden.

2) Now ask the children to brainstorm what they know about composting with a compost pile - without earthworms. Questions you might ask them include:

a) What happens to the temperature during the compost process? It gradually heats up, the temperature peaks, and then declines as the different microorganines do their jobs. The highest temperature reached is about 160 degrees F.

b) What organisms do most of the work in a compost pile community? Microorganisms, such as fungi and bacteria. Macroorganisms (the same creatures that are in the earthworm bin) are also present, *before* and *after* the pile heats up.

c) What ingredients do you put into the compost pile before you start a "run"? Alternate layers of dry and green vegetable matter, and an activator such as manure, blood meal, bone meal, or compost. You could also add lime, soil, and wood ash.

d) What happens to the food waste you put into the compost pile? It is broken down primarily by the action of bacteria and fungi (with some help from macroorganisms) into rich compost.

e) What can you do with the compost that is created after a run? Use it on your garden!

f) What is the best time of year to make a compost pile? Summer and Fall.

(continued)

137

3) We have looked at some of the basic differences between a compost pile and the method used by the Earthworm Compost Farm to break down food waste. **What are some of the most obvious differences?**

- Organisms involved (differences in community)
- Temperatures
- Ingredients
- Time of year

4) If you were a farmer and wanted to compost your food year-round, what sort of system would you set up? Why?

Activity Extensions

🐛 Challenge the children to make **a food web** for the compost column and compost pile, and another for the earthworm bin. Display in classroom.

🐛 Can the children make a web that shows how Earthworm Compost Farming and composting might be connected?

🐛 Make a mural that illustrates the differences and similarities between composting and Earthworm Compost Farming.

Activity 2: Family Activities:

Purpose:

Parents and other family members become involved in the childrens'"earthworm experience". This activity also challenges children to convey to others what they have learned about earthworms.

Procedure:

Children can try any of the following activities at home:

🐛 Encourage the children to invite their parents to **hunt for earthworms.** It is especially fun to go out at night with a flashlight covered with red acetate. For families who want to start an Earthworm Compost Farm, send home instructions on the care and feeding of the worms.

🐛 Have you ever wondered what those delicate dirt dribbles scattered around a grassy area are? They are very likely castings, or the fertile scat of the earthworm. **Looking around the yard or in the park for earthworm castings** and finding their burrow holes is another fun family activity. This entails crawling on hands and knees and exploring hidden surprises in the grass.

🐛 Have the children **construct an earthworm apartment house with their parents.** Send home materials along with a set of questions drawn up by the students. Students can assemble the apartment house with their families and can challenge them with questions about earthworms. It can be exciting to share new knowledge with family members.

Sample Questions for children to ask their parents:

- Why is an earthworm's body moist?
- Does an earthworm have a top and bottom or front and back?
- Are there boy and girl earthworms?
- What do you think earthworms eat?
- What do you think they do in the soil?
- How can we find out?
- What will happen if we put our kitchen scraps into the earth worm column?

🐛 **Create an indoor Earthworm Compost Farm** to recycle kitchen scraps in the home. Hand out a packet for students to take home. This packet can include activities found in chapter 2: Directions for Building an Earthworm Compost Farm, Earthworms in Paradise (needs of earthworms), and Variety of Food Waste Fed to Worms. You might invite interested parents to see the Earthworm Compost Farm in action.

Activity 3: Earth Circle of Life Mural

Purpose:

Children create a mural showing the earthworm's role in the cycle of life.

Materials:

large paper for mural	paints
tape	crayons
scissors	markers

✽ How do earthworms fit into the nutrient cycle? Why are earthworms important to the flow of nutrients? Begin a discussion with the children about how earthworms fit into the nutrient cycle, or into the cycle of life and death. Create a mural that will show the earthworms as being part of the cycle of life. Each student will be able to draw his or her own earthworm on the mural.

Procedure:

1) Pre-cut a large circle from butcher block or poster paper.

2) Tape it onto the wall at the children's eye level.

3) Encourage the children to color or paint the bottom half as soil and the top half as sky.

4) Distribute an earthworm on a moist surface to each child.

5) Have the children draw their earthworm, then have them carefully return the worm to you.

6) Let each child cut out his drawing and tape it onto the soil section of the "Earth Circle of Life Mural".

7) Students can add illustrations of trees, plants, rocks, moss, animals, mushrooms, birds, or insects to the mural. These pictures symbolize the circle of life, within which the earthworms live.

Activity 4: The Earthworm Connection

Purpose:

This activity demonstrates how the origin of everyday things can ultimately be traced back to earthworms.

Materials:

large ball of string
cards (1 card for each student, or pair of students) with everyday
natural items written or drawn on them. Examples can
include milk, wool, pencil, cotton tee-shirt, leather, peanut
butter, maple syrup, paper, ice cream.

> **Note:** Earthworms are responsible for creating fertile soil, which enables plants to grow. Thus any plant or anything that eats plants, as well as the products made from plants and animals, owes its existence to earthworms. In this activity, your students will be creating a web that demonstrates this fact.

Procedure:

1) Ask the children to think of a list of items they use every day. List these on the blackboard. Then challenge them to choose the ones that are natural, not synthetic. Natural items can be human-made but must originally come from a plant or animal. Wool, ice cream, felt, cotton, wood products, paper, peanut butter, butter, cooking oil, food, leather, and books are some examples of natural products. Plastic, nylon, and metal are examples of items that do not come directly from plants or animals.

2) Explain to students that they will be creating a web to show that many things they use are dependent on the earthworm. Each student can choose an item to represent in the web, and write the name of this item on a card.

3) The children, holding their cards, should make a circle with one student in the middle as the "worm". The "worm" will hold many strings that can be linked to the items the children represent.

4) Challenge the children to explain whether or not their product is dependent on earthworms. If it is, they can grab hold of a string that connects them with the worm in the middle. This graphically demonstrates the relationship between the product and the earthworm. (Some children may need guidance in tracing the origin of their product).

5) Now, ask the children what they think would happen if there were no earthworms. Many will say that the products they are familiar with might not exist. Emphasize this by having the earthworm drop all the strings it's holding. The "web" will collapse, demonstrating the important connection to the earthworm.

Activity 5: Crossworm Puzzle

Try the crossworm puzzle to test your vocabulary!

Across
1- Organism that has both sperm and eggs in the same body.

2- Earthworm egg case.

3- Information you are gathering for an experiment.

4- To expose something (i.e. soil) to air.

5- A living plant or animal.

6- Worm manure, also called worm _____.

7- These creatures turn food scraps into soil.

8- Soil mixture of partially decomposed organic waste, bedding, worm castings, cocoons, worms, and other organisms found in the Earthworm Compost Farm.

9- Different parts of the environment - such as temperature, amount of light, food, water, shelter, pollution/cleanliness - that control population growth.

Down
1- A tiny organism that is too small to be seen with the naked eye.

2- Storage sack for food located in the front part of the worm.

3- A kind of substance made from living matter; can be broken down into soil.

4- Part of the worm's digestive system that grinds food up before it moves down the intestine.

5- Slang name for the swollen region on the earthworm.

6- Scientific name for the swollen region on the earthworm.

7- _____ organisms can be seen with the naked eye.

Crossworm words: aerate, clitellum, cocoon, crop, data, hermaphroditic, limiting factors, microorganism, macro, organic, vermicompost, organism, casting, worms, girdle, gizzard.

Crossworm Puzzle

Activity 6: An Assortment of More Culminating Projects

Purpose:

Culminating projects give children a chance to demonstrate what they have learned about the amazing earthworm.

Procedure:

Any of the following projects can be used as student assessment. They are also a wonderful way to celebrate the close of the "Wonderful World of Wigglers".

Life on earth would not be the same without the worm. Celebrate the earthworm's importance in a festive **community event.** Invite students to suggest activities that could take place at this event. Some ideas include skits, puppet shows, video presentations of student projects, hands-on exploration of earthworms, demonstrations of how to build an Earthworm Compost Farm, or selling vermicompost and/or earthworms.

Write a **newspaper story** describing a scenario of what might happen if worms suddenly ceased doing their jobs. Submit it to a local or school newspaper, so others can be alerted to the importance of worms.

From a worm's perspective, draw a **large mural depicting the Cycle of Life** within the soil community.

Create a **pop-up book** that animates the story of the earthworm, plant and soil community.

Construct a **diorama** that contains models of the worms doing their work.

Make a **flip book** that tells the story of the earthworm through animation.

Write a **Life with Earthworms** manual for the community. Topics might include: "How to Build an Earthworm Compost Farm", "An Earthworm's Needs", or "How to Care for Earthworms". Students may also wish to include interesting earthworm facts, explain how earthworms enrich the soil, and demonstrate how earthworms are vital to the ecology of the earth. Ideas for distribution can include local service organizations, gardening clubs, book stores, nurseries, flower shops, or food co-ops.

🐦 Give an **Earthworm Workshop** for the community that includes constructing an Earthworm Compost Farm, raising and caring for worms, and the importance of the worms' role in enriching the soil ecosystem. Or, invite another class and teach them how to set up an Earthworm Compost Farm.

Activity 7: Closure to The Wonderful World of Wigglers

Purpose:

As a culminating discussion, children may form a share circle to express their thoughts about the earthworm. Give the children several minutes to think about what impressed them most about the earthworm. Encourage them to write down their thoughts.

🐛 Share Circle

When all have finished, the children can sit together in a circle, with a bowl of water in the center to moisten hands. One earthworm will be passed from child to child as he takes a turn to share his thoughts and responses to the worm.

The students may preface their thoughts by saying: "I think that the most amazing thing about the earthworm is. . . ."

🐛 Earthworm Pledge

The children can make up a pledge about caring for and respecting earthworms.

A Final Note from Wilma

The following can be read as a letter from Wilma Worm, who introduced the children to the earthworms in Chapter 1.

"Hello everybody! I'm writing to tell you I have moved on to another classroom. I will stay here for a short while to make sure the first meeting between students and earthworms goes smoothly. Remember the first time you met all my relatives? You were wonderful - so kind and gentle and eager to learn about us! I want you to know that I really enjoyed the time I spent with you. Thank you for taking such good care of me, and my relatives! If you have any questions, or would like to write (I love getting mail!), send a letter to the following address, and it will be forwarded to me:"

"Wilma Worm, c/o Food Works, 64 Main Street, Montpelier, Vt. 05602."

Bibliography

Darling, Lois and Louis. *Worms,* William Morrow and Company, New York, NY, 1972.

McLaughlin, Mary. *Earthworms, Dirt and Rotten Leaves: An Exploration In Ecology,* Macmillan Publishing Company, New York, NY, 1986.

Minnich, Jerry. *The Earthworm Book - How to Raise and Use Earthworms for Your Home and Garden,* Rodale Press, Emmaus, PA, 1977.

Pigdon, Keith and Marilyn Woolley. *Earthworms,* Modern Curriculum Press, Cleveland, Ohio, 1989.

Simon, Seymour. *Discovering What Earthworms Do,* McGraw-Hill, New York, NY, 1969.

Appendix

The Earthworm's

EXTERNAL ANATOMY

&

INTERNAL ANATOMY

The Earthworm's
EXTERNAL ANATOMY

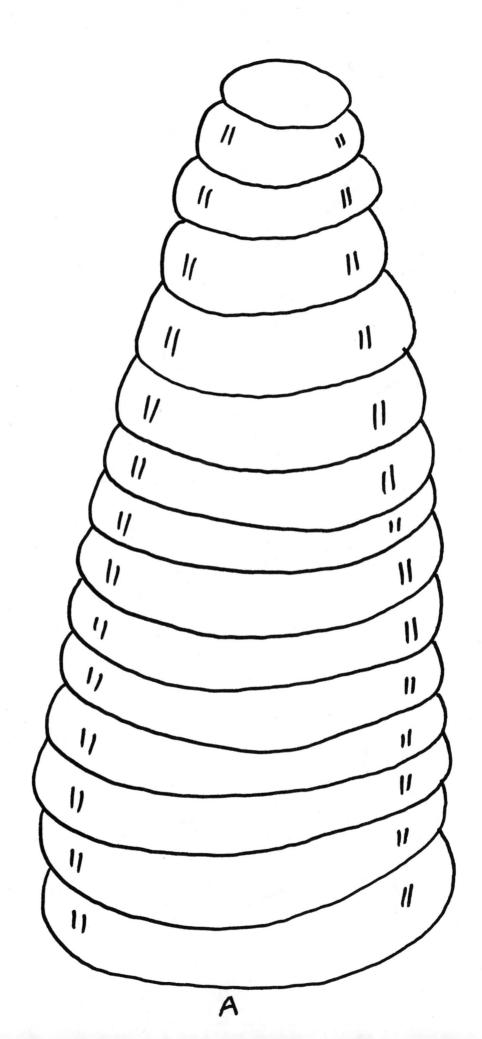

A

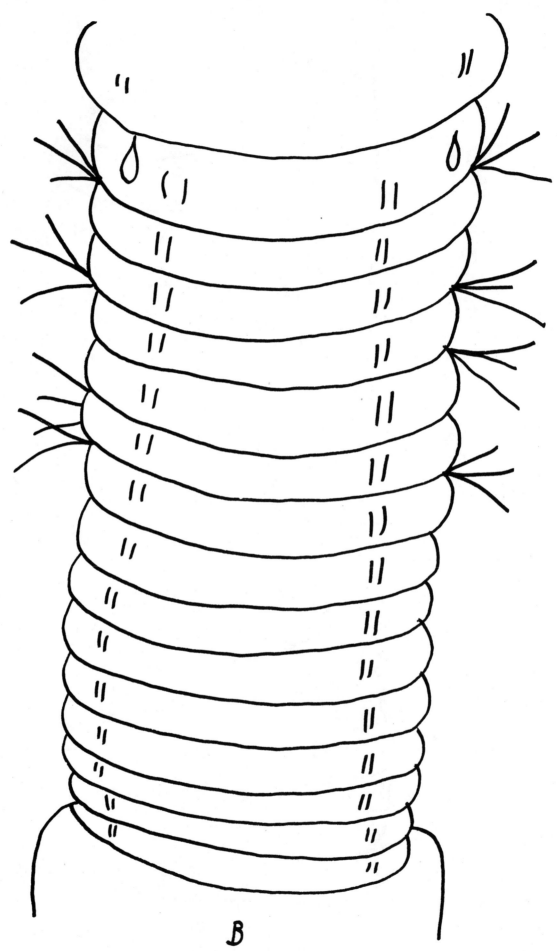

B

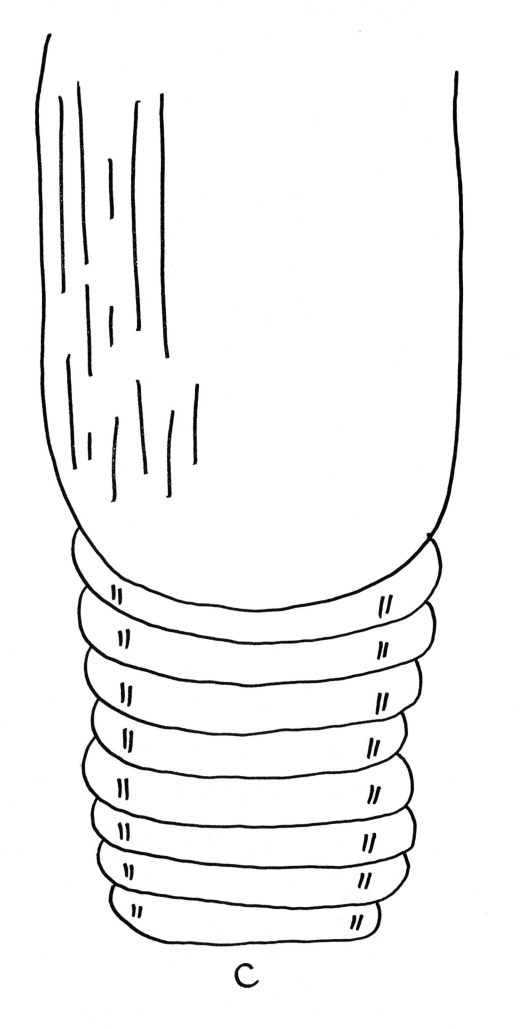

C

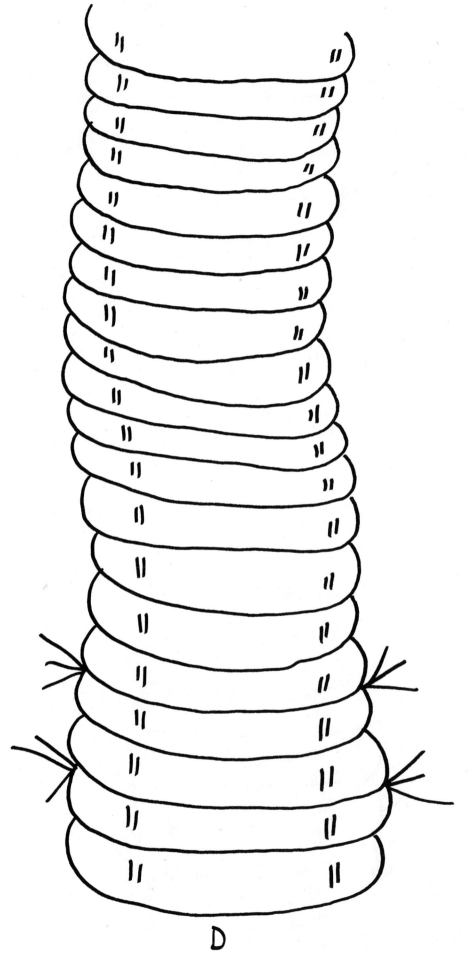

D

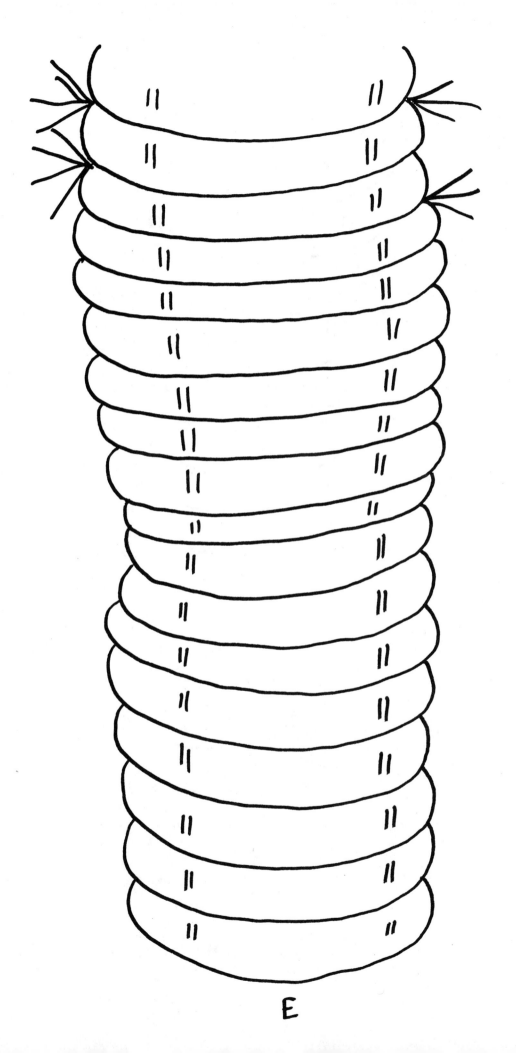

E

F

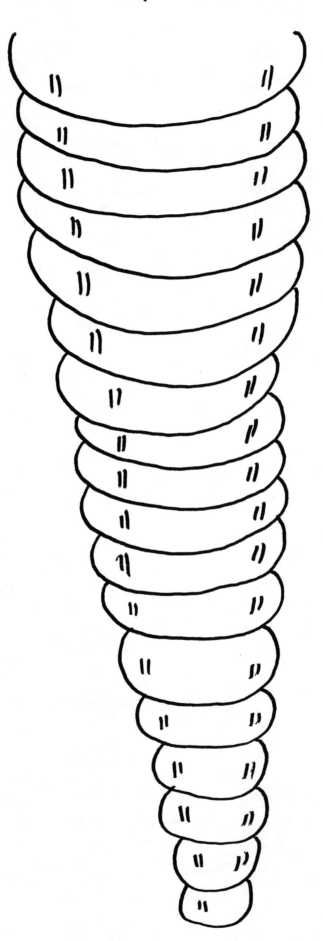

The Earthworm's

INTERNAL ANATOMY

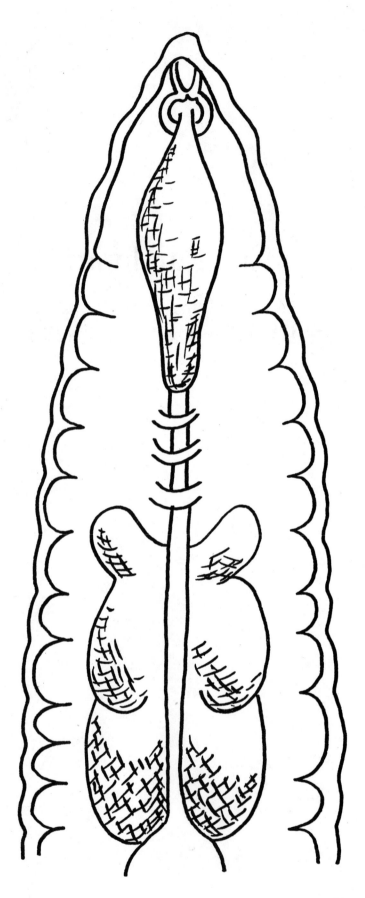

A

B

D

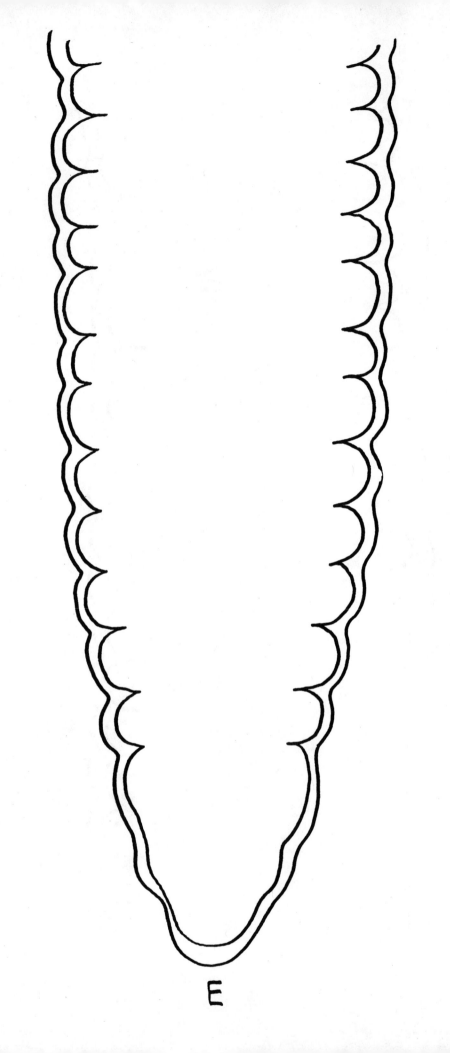

E

The Common Roots Program

Education So Real
You Can See It Growing.

The Food Works *Common Roots* program helps parents, teachers, and other educators develop an integrated curriculum that not only covers practical skills in science, social studies, nutrition, math, writing, and the arts, but also prepares children to confront social and environmental problems in their own communities.

Food Works is an educational organization founded in 1987 to help integrate the themes of food, ecology, and community into elementary school education.

➤ Food Works staff are available for consulting sessions and workshops with teachers, parents and community groups to help integrate the *Common Roots* program.

➤ Food Works staff can visit your group or classroom and present hands-on activities, slideshows, videos, or lectures on themes of food security, ecology, and community service learning.

➤ Food Works has developed a variety of curriculum resource materials for teachers, parents, and community members to use in the classroom. Our K-6 *Common Roots Guidebooks* are an exciting collection of hands-on, hearts-on environmental and historical activities for young learners. Now available are:

"The Wonderful World of Wigglers"	@ $14.95
"Exploring the Forest with Grandforest Tree"	@ $18.95
"Exploring the Secrets of the Meadow-Thicket"	@ $18.95
"In The Three Sisters Garden"	@ $18.95

(add $3.00 s/h per book)

For Complete information regarding the *Common Roots* program or to order additional *Common Roots Guidebooks*, write:

FOOD WORKS
64 Main Street
Montpelier, Vermont 05602
802-229-9433
1-800-310-1515